HOOP HISTORY:

Fifty years of high school boys basketball in Waterbury

VOLUME ONE – 1970 TO 1995

Michael Griffin

Printed in the United States of America

First Printing, 2021

ISBN: 978-0-578-92850-0

Library of Congress Control Number: 2021923106

Credit for cover graphic: iStock.com/Enterline Design Services LLC

Highbury Press
P.O. Box 3447
Waterbury, CT 06705-3447

www.highburypress.com

This book is dedicated to my parents:

For my father, who took me to countless high school games during my youth, and sparked an interest in the sport and in the history of Waterbury.

For my mother, whose interest in this – as in all of my endeavors – was never less than my own.

Thank you for all of your support.

Acknowledgements

There may be only one person's name on the cover of this book, but the final product would not have been possible without the help of many individuals who provided assistance along the way.

I would first like to thank a number of former high school coaches for being receptive to my idea/plan for the book. The enthusiastic response and assistance from Jack Taglia, Ed Generali, Nick Augelli and Bob Brown not only provided wonderful anecdotes for the book but served as an impetus to keep working through tough times during the pandemic.

Athletic directors at Waterbury's high schools provided valuable information throughout the duration of the project. Thank you to Dave Ieronimo of Crosby, Alan Piccolo at Wilby, Dave Rossi of Kennedy, Mike Madden at Sacred Heart and Jerry Ciarleglio and Mike Giampetruzzi of Holy Cross.

Thanks also to Marty Morra, former scorekeeper for Sacred Heart, who has compiled a wealth of statistical information on the Hearts' basketball program. And thank you to Ned Conlan, a former teacher at Crosby who offered a look at some of his own collection of hoops history to contribute to the book.

A number of former players have graciously shared their memories and experiences from their playing days. Thank you to Frank Samuelson, Clay Johnson, Carmen Giampetruzzi, Dewey Stinson, Matt Mariani, Harold Miller and Edmund Saunders of Holy Cross. Thank you to Pete Anton, Al Piccolo, Willie Davis and Ryan Sullivan of Crosby. Thank you to Jay Seay, Phil Lott and James "Manny" Wright of Wilby. Thank you to Gary Franks of Sacred Heart, Hank Spellman of Kaynor Tech and Malik Williams and Garrett Petteway of Kennedy.

Republican-American newsroom librarian Mike DeGirolamo offered his expertise relating to the newspaper's archives. Thank you to Mike along with managing editor Anne Karolyi and photographer Jim Shannon – also from the Republican-American.

To the staffers at the reference desk at Silas Bronson Library in Waterbury, thank you for help in accessing years and years of newspapers on microfilm, along with old high school yearbooks on file, that provided the bulk of the statistics, game reports and photos reprised in the book.

Thank you to Diane Ciba, an instructor with OLLI-UConn, whose course helped push the idea for such a book into a full-fledged, working project.

To Julie Broad and the Book Launchers team, thank you for some timely tips on various aspects of the writing and publishing process.

Thank you to my parents, sisters and brother for being a sounding board of sorts as I worked through stages of the book process.

Thanks to you all; you have helped to turn what began as a fanciful idea into a years-long endeavor that aims to preserve some sports history while hopefully enlightening readers along the way.

– Michael Griffin

Contents

1970s

Contents

1980s

Contents

1990s

Introduction

I t is not uncommon to hear sports fans recount their first trip to a famous stadium, relating the emotions experienced as part of that initial visit to a place they now consider sacred ground.

For many in these parts of southern New England, such an event usually revolves around a major league baseball game at Yankee Stadium in New York or Boston's Fenway Park.

I grew up a New York Mets fan and was lucky enough to see a World Series game on my first trip to a major league stadium as a seven-year-old, when the Mets played the Oakland A's at Shea Stadium on a cold October night in 1973.

That experience certainly left an impression on me as a young child; I still have the ticket stub to the game tucked away in a bedroom dresser drawer as a way of preserving the memory … even though my love for the Mets has faded over the years in much the same fashion as the ink and graphics on that cherished souvenir.

I received another keepsake related to a different sport that same year that also remains in my possession; it is representative of a passion sparked those many years ago that has grown over time and serves as inspiration for this book.

That winter of 1973-74 marked the first season that my father began taking me along with him to see high school basketball games in Waterbury, and I began rooting for Crosby High as my mother – a math teacher at Crosby – taught a number of the players on the team.

She gave me a white wooden ruler imprinted with Crosby's 1973-74 boys basketball schedule (the well-worn back side of which is shown below). The ruler served me well as a homework aid for a number of school years while my interest in that school's team and my desire to attend games between city schools grew and grew.

Those first high school games I attended were all played at Kennedy High School. It was built in the mid-1960s and had taken over from the Waterbury Armory as host site for scholastic hoop contests in the city, as the older schools' gymnasiums were not sufficient to accommodate certain size crowds at the time.

The Armory had itself been a famed venue for many city sports fans, drawing crowds of a couple thousand who would congregate for basketball doubleheaders during the winter sports seasons of the 1940s, 1950s and early 1960s.

The likes of Bob Markovic, Dick

		CROSBY HIGH SCHOOL —
Dec. 7 Watertown	Away	Jan. 4 Wilby
Dec. 11 Holy Cross	Home	Jan. 8 Warren H
Dec. 15 Torrington	Away	Jan. 12 Sacred He
Dec. 19 Wilcox Tech	Home	Jan. 15 Watertown
Dec. 21 Naugatuck	Home	Jan. 18 West Have
Dec. 26 Wolcott	Away	Jan. 22 Warren He
Dec. 28 Kennedy	Home	Jan. 25 Kennedy

Clary and Billy Finn were among the stars who delighted the crowds with their basketball brilliance while teams from Leavenworth, Wilby and Sacred Heart gained city glory by capturing state or New England titles during that period.

The movement of games to Kennedy in the mid-1960s began a historical transition for scholastic basketball in the city, as the Town Plot school was the first of four new high school buildings built within a decade and a half that each had new gymnasiums to host their teams and the dedicated fan base associated with each.

Holy Cross High School opened its doors as an all-boys school on Oronoke Road in Waterbury in 1968, and had a varsity basketball program in place by the 1970-71 school year.

Crosby High would have a new home and its own impressive gym (nicknamed "The Palace") in 1974, when the school moved from downtown Waterbury to a modern complex on Pierpont Road.

And by the end of the 1970s, Wilby High had followed Crosby's move to the outskirts of the city by taking up residence at a new site in the North End.

The Armory era may have been over, but high school hoopsters would continue to thrill local followers who attended games or listened to WATR radio broadcasts of city and Naugatuck Valley League (NVL) contests.

The Waterbury schools extended their dominance of the NVL into this new era; a city team would win or gain a share of the conference title in all but three of the 50 seasons from 1970-71 through 2019-20.

Each of the five high schools in Waterbury claimed an NVL crown during the first five years of that period – a remarkable stat that served as an indication of the balance of power and talent spread throughout the city as the modern game began to flourish.

The biggest scholastic stars of the 1970s included Tony Hanson, who led Holy Cross to an undefeated regular season in 1973 – the first time a city team had accomplished that feat in 50 years – and Steve Johnson, who sparked Crosby's surge to prominence in the middle of that decade.

The 1980s saw Waterbury join New Haven, Bridgeport and Hartford as the top hotbeds for high school basketball in Connecticut, evidenced by four different city schools reaching state title games over a short two-year span (the 1981-82 and 1982-83 seasons).

Sacred Heart won the CIAC Class M basketball title the following year, the first of 13 state crowns for city schools between 1984 and 2017.

Each of the five city schools in the NVL have enjoyed periods atop city and league standings since that 1984 campaign, as the game continued to evolve.

S" — 1973-74 BASKETBALL

Home	Jan. 29	Wolcott		Home
Away	Feb. 1	Holy Cross		Away
Away	Feb. 6	Naugatuck		Away
Home	Feb. 8	Torrington		Home
Away	Feb. 12	Bullard Haven		Home
Home	Feb. 15	Sacred Heart		Home
Away	Feb. 21	Wilby		Away

The three-point shot was instituted for CIAC competition by the end of the 1980s, and Phil Lott of Wilby became the first 2,000-point scorer in city history as the Wildcats fielded some of their strongest teams in modern times.

The 1990s began with Kennedy the dominant squad in the NVL. The Eagles claimed three consecutive league titles from 1989 through 1991, marking the first time that any school had accomplished that feat in over 50 years.

The inside-out duo of Harold Miller and Edmund Saunders paced Holy Cross to a state title in 1995. The Crusaders would go on to claim their third CIAC crown in 2000.

And since the turn of the century, two programs have sustained long runs at or near the top.

Coach Nick Augelli's Crosby squads won 10 of the 11 NVL titles between 2004 and 2014. The Bulldogs appeared in five state championship finals – winning three – between 1998 and 2008, with Julian Allen (in 2005) and B.J. Monteiro (2008) earning Connecticut Player of the Year honors.

Jon Carroll's Sacred Heart teams captured four straight CIAC championships from 2014 through 2017 – with star guard Mustapha Heron leading the team for three of those years – part of a run of five consecutive NVL tournament wins).

The recent Bulldog and Hearts teams have raised the city's game to a higher level, completing half a century of transformation from the city's Armory days when the game was generally played much closer to the floor.

As the game moved "above the rim," the floors of those four city high school gyms built in the 1960s and '70s have also changed – in name, as recognition for coaches who made a lasting impression on their players and on the city's sports scene

Kennedy' High's home floor is now called Jack Taglia Court, named for the former coach who guided the Eagles to those consecutive titles amid his many years at the helm.

Wilby High's gym has been renamed Reggie O'Brien Court, for the man who directed some of the school's best-ever teams, during the 1980s and 1990s.

The floor of the Crosby Palace is now officially called Coach Nick Augelli Court. Augelli has spent 50-plus years on the Bulldog sidelines, 42 as head coach, and has more than 700 wins over his career – a total that places him second all-time in victories among high school coaches in Connecticut.

And players at Holy Cross now perform on Ed Generali Court at Tim McDonald Gymnasium, in honor of the men who coached the Crusaders to a total of three state titles and numerous

Crosby players stand with coach Nick Augelli during the 2015 ceremony held to rename the school's basketball court in his honor.

league championships on that floor.

These local gymnasiums may not rival Madison Square Garden or Yankee Stadium as world-renowned sports venues, but the legacy created by the honored coaches and their talented teams at each site has certainly left their mark on Waterbury sports fans – some of whom may even consider these local courts as sacred ground.

As you read through the following pages in this first of two volumes that together will detail the accomplishments of city teams over the past 50 years, here's hoping that you'll recall the first high school basketball games that you attended, and the accompanying memories that might still remain.

The 1970s

Contributed / Holy Cross High School

Tony Hanson of Holy Cross puts up a shot in a Crusaders' home game during the 1971-72 season.

1970-71: Franks leads Hearts to title; Holy Cross starts varsity program

The words may seem a bit strange to read now, but a story in the sports section of the *Waterbury Republican* on December 8, 1970, began with the following paragraph:

"The unusual arrangement of having three Waterbury high school basketball teams playing at home in three different gymnasiums – which could very well be a first – is on the agenda for tonight."

Believe it or not, there was a time not long ago when some of the city's schools did not have their own spiffy gymnasiums expansive enough to accommodate crowds of even a decent size to watch a high school game.

As Bob Palmer, Jr. would go on to explain in his newspaper article previewing the slate of games for that December evening half a century ago, the 1970-71 season marked the start of a new era of sorts for the city's high school basketball scene – with Holy Cross High competing on the varsity level for the first time in the school's third year of operation.

The Crusaders had played their first-ever varsity game one week earlier on December 1, 1970, losing on the road at East Catholic of Manchester, and had hosted Kennedy in their first city contest in their new gym on December 5.

Kennedy prevailed on that historic occasion, which came four days after the Eagles captured the city jamboree – defeating Wilby in the final period by a 35-34 scoreline. Senior guard Carmen Vaccarelli scored 16 points in the championship period for Kennedy, whose win broke a streak of six consecutive victories by Sacred Heart in the traditional sea-son-opening event for city schools.

Sacred Heart, the defending city and Naugatuck Valley League champion, featured star guard /forward Gary Franks and 6-4 Paul Gillis among a group of returning players aiming to repeat as title holders.

Wilby represented the main threat to dethrone the Hearts. Captains Tom Weaver and John Greco were among the key returnees for coach Jack Delaney's Wildcats squad that also included Larry Chapman and Tom Dupont.

Like Holy Cross, the Hearts opened the regular season with a non-league loss to perennial state power East Catholic. But the team rebounded quickly to put together another fine season under coach John Gilmore. Pete Eason emerged as a consistent double-figure scorer to complement Franks, and Sacred Heart went 12-2 in league games to claim a second consecutive NVL crown.

The 6-1 Franks averaged 28.8 points per game to lead Sacred Heart. He scored a career-high 48 points in an overtime loss to East Catholic later that season, and notched 36 points and 20-plus rebounds against Kennedy.

Wilby finished second to the Hearts in the NVL standings with an 11-3 record. The Wildcats closed with four straight wins that included a come-from-behind win over Crosby in the final regular-season contest that kept the Bulldogs from qualifying for the state tournament. Tom Dupont paced the victorious Wildcats with 26 points and 17 rebounds; Fred Sheppard notched 30 points for Crosby, which ended the

The 1970-71 All-City team included three Wilby players – Tom Weaver, Larry Chapman and Tom Dupont – along with Gary Franks of Sacred Heart and Crosby's Fred Sheppard.

campaign with a 10-10 overall record.

Kennedy qualified for the Class AA tournament by defeating Sacred Heart in its final regular-season game to finish with a 10-9 record. Eagles' big man Bill Eason poured in 30 points in the 90-87 win.

The victory earned Kennedy a game against Manchester in the playdown round of the Class AA tournament. The back-and-forth affair went down down to the closing seconds, until Manchester's Bill People scored with four seconds left to break a 80-80 tie and end the Waterbury team's season. Carmen Vaccarelli netted 23 points and the 6-5 Eason added

20 for Kennedy.

Wilby defeated New Canaan 69-65 in the playdown round to advance to a matchup against Notre Dame of Bridgeport in the first round of the Class A tournament. Trailing by double digits in the opening period, the Wildcats rallied to take the lead. But Notre Dame's Jerome Lademan scored 10 of his 40 points in the final period to lead the Lancers to an 80-66 victory. Larry Chapman netted 19 points for Wilby while Tom Weaver added 17 in the loss.

Sacred Heart, rated 14th in the Class A tourney, opened an early lead against Windsor Locks in its playdown contest, and led by a 36-32 margin at the half. Their 24th-seeded opponents outscored the Hearts 20-8 in the third period and held on for a 69-64 win, ending the Hearts' season at 14-7.

Franks, who surpassed 1,000 career points in his senior season and would go on to play at Yale, made history by becoming the first person to claim both the Billy Finn Award (as outstanding player among city seniors) and the Doc McInerney Award (as top scholar-athlete in the city). The honors were awarded on the final night of the regular season along with the Lt. Jack Cullinan Award for sportsmanship, which went to Kennedy's Tom Kirvin.

The All-City team, voted on by coaches of the six city high schools, featured three players who were repeat selections: Chapman and Weaver of Wilby and Franks of Sacred Heart. A third Wilby player, Tom Dupont, and Crosby's Fred Sheppard rounded out the all-star squad.

Contributed / Holy Cross High School

Action from an NVL contest at the Holy Cross gym, which hosted its first varsity games during the 1970-71 season.

Looking Back: Sacred Heart's Franks made an impact on and off the court

Sacred Heart High School's storied basketball history includes nine CIAC state titles and numerous players who have earned All-State honors since the program was started in 1940.

But one of the school's best-ever performers nearly enrolled in another city high school his freshman year. Gary Franks — the All-State swingman who helped lead the Hearts to back-to-back Naugatuck Valley League titles before starring at Yale University and later making history by becoming the first Black Republican Congressman in nearly 60 years — was set to start high school at Kennedy High in the fall of 1967 after graduating from Tinker Elementary School.

"My parents and siblings wanted me to go to Taft Prep School (in Watertown). I interviewed there but was rejected," says Franks. "So, it looked like I was going to Kennedy when my sister decided to have me meet with Father Blanchfield (the principal at Sacred Heart)."

Having missed the admissions test earlier in the year, Franks' nearly straight-A's report card from Tinker impressed Blanchfield enough to earn him a place in Sacred Heart's freshman class.

While the meeting paved the way for Franks to attend the city parochial school, he wasn't unfamiliar with Sacred Heart and its basketball program. As an eighth-grader, he had followed the exploits of the 1966-67 Hearts team that captured city and NVL titles and then claimed the CIAC Class L crown, the first state title for a Waterbury school in 14 years.

"I was able to go to every Sacred Heart tournament game that year, thanks to my seventh-grade teacher who was a SHHS grad," remembers Franks. "I listened to nearly every game on WATR during the regular season and I felt like I knew the entire team.

"Well, I did know one player — Joel Goldson, who was a neighbor of mine when I lived near Orange Street. He was one of the many legends out of Walsh School, who dominated the City Grade School League back in the day (before middle schools were instituted, when each elementary school included kindergarten through eighth grades)."

Franks would himself dominate city and NVL hoop contests — averaging over 20 points per game in his junior year and nearly 29 ppg in his final season — and helped to lead Sacred Heart to three city championships and back-to-back Naugatuck Valley League titles during his scholastic career.

"I had an outstanding high school coach — John Gilmore — who managed to get the best and most out of his teams," says Franks. "We had

Gary Franks of Sacred Heart.

a humble cockiness to each of our teams. And, we worked hard in each and every practice."

The 6-1 Franks earned second-team All-State status from the New Haven Register as a junior, before making first team All-State as a senior in 1971. "I was ranked as the top senior in New England that year by Cage World (the basketball publication that covered the scholastic game in the Northeast)," he recalls.

His decision to attend Yale University was influenced by a desire to follow the path of one of his idols growing up. "Bill Bradley was my role model when I was in grade school; he was at Princeton and I wanted to go to an Ivy League college as well," notes Franks.

"I too never wanted to be known as just a basketball player or even the best high school player ever. I wanted to be the best scholar-athlete ever," adds Franks, whose senior-year honors reflected that pursuit.

He was recipient of both the Billy Finn Award (top senior player) and Doc McInerney Award (top scholar-athlete) in 1971, becoming the first player to earn those two honors given to Waterbury seniors after each scholastic season.

It was an achievement that would have impressed Bill Bradley. And, as fate would have it, many years later Sen. Bill Bradley and Congressman Gary Franks would serve in Congress together.

But before that, Franks had a stellar career at Yale that earned him invitations to rookie camps by a few NBA teams after his senior season. Opting for a tryout with the New Orleans Jazz, "I was the last rookie cut that year — cut by Elgin Baylor," says Franks, who was encouraged to play in the Continental Basketball Assocation.

He instead opted for the business world, working for some Fortune 500 companies and eventually presiding over a real estate management firm.

Franks served as a member of the Waterbury board of aldermen from 1986 to 1990, when he was elected to the U.S. House of Representatives. A Congressional pioneer, he was the first Black Congressman from New England and the first Republican voting member of the Congressional Black Caucus.

During his time in Washington (from 1991 to 1997), Congressman Franks helped to bring a record amount of defense contracts to Connecticut, chaired the GOP effort on welfare reform, worked on civil rights legislation and fought to end racial gerrymandering. He served on the Armed Services, Energy and Commerce Committees.

After his political career, he established his own public affairs firm, was a visiting professor at Georgetown University, University of Virginia, Hampton University, and wrote three political books.

Franks' achievements are indicative of a family full of high achievers. Coming from humble beginnings, he is one of six children raised by diligent, loving parents, with each succeeding "through hard work and the grace of God," he notes.

"Three of my siblings hold doctorate degrees, one brother became a Colonel in the Army, and another brother was a grade school teacher and coach," adds Franks, who has certainly fulfilled his early ambitions to succeed on and off the basketball court.

1971-72: Kennedy claims city, NVL championships for first time

With Sacred Heart having graduated four starters from the previous year's team, other city squads were poised to claim city and NVL bragging rights from the Hearts for the 1971-72 basketball season.

Kennedy – featuring an experienced side led by co-captains Bill Eason and Fred Petteway along with guard Chuck Giorgio – started the league campaign in strong fashion and maintained a narrow gap ahead of public school rivals Crosby and Wilby as the season progressed.

The sharp-shooting Rich Reid – who averaged 20 points per game on the season – and big man Rodney Parker kept Crosby in the running before losing two games in a row late in the season, giving Kennedy a chance to clinch the NVL title on the road against Torrington.

The 6-5 Eason tallied 36 points and 17 rebounds and Giorgio scored 17 as coach Marty Sweeney's Eagles claimed an 80-66 victory over the Red Raiders to earn the school its first-ever league crown. Kennedy went on to finish with a 12-2 NVL record, two games ahead of second-place Crosby.

After an 8-3 start to the season, Wilby needed to defeat Naugatuck in its second-to-last NVL game to qualify for the state tournament. Tom Dupont scored a season-high 28 points and four teammates also hit double figures in the 86-78 win for Wilby, which became the fifth city team that year to qualify for CIAC play – a first-ever feat for Waterbury schools.

Wilby brought a 10-9 record into its Class A playdown game against Warren Harding of Bridgeport. The Governors' size and speed proved too much for the Wildcats, who were eliminated with the 89-67 result.

Harding advanced to play Crosby in the next round, a closer contest that went down to the final buzzer. Harding built an early lead before Rodney Parker sparked a Crosby comeback. Down by one with the ball in the closing seconds,

Contributed / Kennedy High School

Wilby's Tom Dupont, recipient of the Billy Finn Award in 1972, releases a shot in a game at Kennedy that season.

Crosby's Rich Reid launched a corner jumper that bounded off the rim as time expired, ending the Bulldogs' season.

Holy Cross, playing an independent schedule and still a year away from joining the NVL, compiled a 13-7 record – one year after going 2-18 in the school's initial varsity season – to earn the school its first appearance in the CIAC tournament.

The Crusaders' initial tourney game was a victorious one, with senior Ray White collecting 25 points and 15 rebounds in a 76-65 decision over Shelton in a Class A playdown game, to earn a matchup against city foe Kennedy.

Having lost twice to the Eagles in the regular season, Holy Cross recovered from a 9-0 deficit to cruise past Kennedy, 81-61, in the tourney contest. White and junior Tony Hanson combined for 41 Crusader points while Ollie Jones led Kennedy with 15 points in the team's final game.

The Crusaders then faced another team it had played twice during the season in the Class A quarterfinals. Having split regular-season games with East Catholic, Holy Cross fell to the Manchester side by a 74-47 margin. The 6-4 Hanson, who would be selected for the All-State team for Class A, scored 19 points in the loss.

Marty Sweeney, coach at Kennedy High.

Bill Eason of Kennedy, who went on to enjoy a fine career at Providence College.

Kaynor Tech, the city's technical school that competed in the Mattatuck Regional Conference, was also among the Waterbury high schools to reach the CIAC tournament in 1972. Led by guard Larry Dawson, who earned All-State status the previous season, the Panthers topped Stonington, 80-69, in its Class B opener before falling to Montville in the next round and finishing the season with a 14-8 record.

Dupont of Wilby and Kennedy's Eason helmed the All-City and All-NVL squads. Joining the pair on the All-City team were Eason's Kennedy teammate Giorgio, along with Crosby's Reid and Hanson of Holy Cross.

Dupont – who averaged 18.5 points and 17 rebounds per outing – was honored with the Billy Finn Award as the top senior player in the city, and he shared the Doc McInerney Award (as top scholar athlete) with White of Holy Cross. Reid of Crosby claimed the Jack Cullinan Award for sportsmanship among city seniors.

The All-NVL team included Dupont, Reid, Pete Eason of Sacred Heart, Willie McFarland of Ansonia and Kennedy's Eason, who scored at a 22.8 points-per-game clip for the 1971-72 season before heading off to prep school.

23

1965 opening of Kennedy's gym marked 'the future of NVL basketball'

... and became a special home for one attendee at the venue's initial event

Kennedy High's 1972 NVL boys basketball title was the first league crown for the school that opened in September of 1965 and began serving as the main venue for hoop contests involving Waterbury schools.

Now – decades later – the Eagles' home court may no longer be the city's biggest or fanciest venue among several high school sites. But its opening more than half a century ago served as a landmark for Waterbury sports that helped spark a transition from the storied Armory era into the modern age for high school basketball in Waterbury.

The gym was officially dedicated on Dec. 6, 1965, with a ceremony involving Waterbury dignitaries prior to the annual Waterbury High School Jamboree that included teams from Crosby, Kennedy, Sacred Heart and Wilby.

Among the many fans in attendance that opening night was the man whose name is now synonymous with the gymnasium. Jack Taglia, who would go on to coach for 31 seasons at Kennedy and lead the Eagles to three NVL titles, was a Sacred Heart sophomore and member of the Hearts' junior varsity team at the time.

"I was certainly there for that jamboree and I remember that the Kennedy gym was state-of-the-art compared to the Armory," says Taglia. "Because the four city teams played there, there was a game almost every night of the week. Since I lived within walking distance to Kennedy, I was there for many of those early games."

The following season, Sacred Heart, playing most of its games at Kennedy, was NVL champion and produced

Reprinted with permission of the Republican-American

Ed Hill of Crosby drives to the hoop as teammate Bob Guerrera screens out Don Valdez of Kennedy in action during the 1965 city jamboree, the first event staged at the Kennedy gym.

a memorable run through the CIAC tournament to claim the state title. Paul Zorsky, 6-7 Don Sasso and playmaker Joe Summa led a deep Hearts team under coach John Gilmore that finished 20-3 and defeated Fairfield Prep for the 1967 Class L crown.

"The one game that does stand out that year was when we beat Hillhouse High at Kennedy in the first game of the season," says Taglia. "I don't ever remember from the Armory days that a Waterbury team ever beat a New Haven team."

Kennedy would continue to host most city contests through the mid-70s (prior to the new Crosby High being built). And the host school's fans finally got to cheer an NVL title of their own when guard Chuck Giorgio and 6-5 sophomore Bill Eason led the team to a 12-2 record in the league in 1971-72.

That team was coached by Marty Sweeney, who Taglia replaced as head coach in 1977. "And in my first couple of years, wins were hard to come by," admits Taglia. "I coached because I loved the game and I loved working with my players and watching them evolve into a team."

The dedication and perseverance would pay off a decade later, when Kennedy claimed three straight NVL titles between 1989 through 1991.

"The most memorable game that I ever coached was when we beat Wilby in the last game of the year in front of a standing room crowd for my first league championship as a coach. I had been coaching 12 years up to that point and I had my doubts that I would ever be involved in a league championship," says Taglia. "Playing in a state championship game certainly is right up there, but winning the first league title was really something special."

Two more NVL titles would follow,

Contributed / Kennedy High School

Former Kennedy coach Jack Taglia thanks friends, family and former players during a dedication of the gymnasium in his name in January 2013.

along with that appearance in the Class M title game in 1990, with Jerome Malloy, Malik Williams and Garnett Petteway leading his most talented team. Taglia would go on to guide the Eagles through the 2007-08 season.

In 2013, the Kennedy High gym was renamed Jack Taglia Gymnasium.

Among the speakers at the ceremony to honor Taglia was retired Torrington coach Tony Turina, who provided some historical perspective on the venue. Turina mentioned that when city basketball moved out of the old Armory and into the newly built Kennedy High gym, "it was like Madison Square Garden. The new gym took the place of the Armory, and it was the beginning of the future for NVL basketball."

Taglia considers "the dedication of the Kennedy gym in my name the most humbling honor I've ever received as a coach, by far. It is not something that ever crossed my mind or that I aspired to while I was coaching."

And surely not something that crossed his mind over half a century ago, the first time he entered the Kennedy High gymnasium, to attend its opening event.

1972-73: Holy Cross makes history in its first season in NVL

Holy Cross High School joined the Naugatuck Valley League for the 1972-73 school year, with expectations high for its basketball team that featured an experienced group of seniors, led by All-State forward Tony Hanson, and 6-6 sophomore Jim Abromaitis.

Considered among the favorites to win the league in that inaugural season, the Crusaders accomplished the feat in historic fashion, becoming the first city team to complete an undefeated regular season in more than 50 years — dating back to the 1921-22 run of Crosby's squad.

Hanson scored 31 points in an opening-night victory over Wilby. Fellow senior Jim Albon then matched that individual point total in an 88-54 rout of Crosby, as the Crusaders began the season in impressive fashion.

A romp over a 2-0 Sacred Heart team followed, before both Kennedy and Naugatuck tried to slow the pace against Holy Cross in early-season contests. Naugatuck even had a one-point lead in the final minute, but foul shots by Hanson and Albon provided a 56-53 victory.

Gaining momentum — and a following among sports fans in the city — as the season progressed, Holy Cross claimed its biggest win of the season by defeating Hartford Public, the top-ranked team in Connecticut, by a 75-69 margin. The host Crusaders gained control after an even first half, and the 6-4 Hanson finished with 29 points and 17 rebounds.

The do-it-all senior reached the

Contributed / Holy Cross High School

Tony Hanson (right) in action during the 1972-73 season.

1,000-point mark for his career three games later in a win over Crosby, combining with senior point guard Mark Duquette for 40 points on the night.

Victories over Torrington and Watertown followed, giving Holy Cross the Naugatuck Valley League title, but Duquette broke his right wrist in the Watertown game and would not play for the rest of the season.

Albon and Hanson combined for 57 points to help dispatch Naugatuck, leaving a trio of games against non-league opponents, including two-time defending state champion in East Catholic of Manchester, to be maneuvered for Holy Cross to complete a perfect regular-season mark.

The Crusader frontline held strong against East Catholic, as Hanson recorded 33 points and 15 rebounds, 6-5 Dennis McGuire scored 12 and sophomore Abromaitis pulled down 21 rebounds in a 66-60 victory.

Next up was high-scoring Larry Kelley and New Haven's Lee High in the 19th game of the season. Kelley may have outdueled Hanson, 37 points to 35, in a personal scoring battle but Holy Cross won the war. The Crusaders responded to a late Lee rally by scoring the final seven points of the game in the 79-71 win.

Holy Cross completed its 20-0 regular season by wining, 64-47, over Notre Dame of West Haven. McGuire and Hanson combined for 37 points as the Crusaders pulled away, in a contest that was tied at halftime, to finish off its historic feat in front of an energetic home crowd.

The Crusaders were rewarded with the top seed in the CIAC Class LL tournament, but the loss of point guard Duquette to injury proved to be a tough hurdle to overcome in the state playoffs.

Contributed / Holy Cross High School

Holy Cross senior guard Jim Albon takes a jump shot over an opponent.

Jim Albon led the way in the CIAC opener, scoring 19 in Holy Cross' 74-58 win over Hall of West Hartford. Abromaitis notched 15 points and a season-high 26 rebounds and Hanson scored 17 while playing with an injured ankle.

Holy Cross faced Fitch of Groton in the Class LL quarterfinals, with key reserve Paul O'Bear joining Duquette on the sidelines due to an illness. The pressure defense of Fitch got to Holy

Cross early, giving the Groton side a ten-point lead in the first period.

Hanson and Albon sparked a Holy Cross comeback, and the Crusaders surged to a 32-31 lead at the break. But with Abromaitis in foul trouble, Fitch regained the lead in the third period and would hold on to eliminate Holy Cross, 64-57. Hanson scored 27 and Albon had 21 in their final high-school games.

"I'm disappointed that we lost, but I'm not disappointed in the kids. They have no reason to be ashamed," coach Tim McDonald told the *Waterbury Republican* after the game. "No one can take this season away from us. The kids worked hard for four years and it paid off this year."

Three other city teams qualified for the 1973 state tournament, all claiming an initial win before falling to higher-ranked opponents.

Wilby defeated Bristol Central, 60-55, in a Class L playdown game, behind 21 points from Jim Arline and 16 from Lou Canady. The Wildcats then lost to Warren Harding of Bridgeport, the third seed, by a 62-53 margin after leading by double digits at halftime.

Kennedy, the #13 seed in Class L, opened tourney play with a 72-55 win over Xavier, with 6-1 guard Chuck Giorgio leading the way with 21 points. The Eagles took East Haven to overtime in the next round, but were eliminated, 71-69. Center Pop Baskins scored 21 and Giorgio added 15 in the loss.

Sacred Heart won its opener in Class S, but the 16th-seeded Hearts were then defeated, 51-44, by top-seeded St. Thomas Aquinas of New Britain. Bob Moffo netted 17 points and Pete Eason scored 12 in the Hearts' finale.

Sacred Heart's Eason and Moffo were selected to the all-NVL team, along with Hanson of Holy Cross, Lou Canady of Wilby and Kennedy's Giorgio.

Hanson, an All-State pick for a second time who was widely considered the top player in New England, was named winner of the Billy Finn Award as the top senior in the city. Pete Eason was recipient of the Jack Cullinan award for sportsmanship, and Crosby's Mike Carter was honored as top scholar-athlete with the Doc McInerney Award.

Contributed / Holy Cross High School

Seniors on Holy Cross' 1972-73 team: Kneeling, left to right, Jim Albon, Paul O'Bear, Mark Duquette; Standing, left to right, Dennis McGuire, Tony Hanson, Stan Zaksewicz, Frank Samuelson.

Looking Back: HC's Frank Samuelson remembers early years, title season

The Holy Cross gymnasium hosted its first varsity basketball game on Dec. 5, 1970, a 76-70 loss to Kennedy. The Crusaders, who held a fourth-quarter lead but were outscored 13 to 5 over the final three minutes of a back-and-forth affair, were led by Tom Amodeo's 14 points while sophomores Mark Duquette and Tony Hanson also reached double figures.

"We were a young team, mainly a bunch of sophomores having to play most games against guys who were a couple of years older than us," remembers Frank Samuelson about that initial season at Holy Cross. "Coach (Tim) McDonald and Assistant Coach (Marty) DeFazio realized we'd take our lumps for a year or so, but knew it would help us build for successive seasons."

Frank Samuelson

The Crusaders endured a 2-18 opening campaign in the new gym, but it wasn't long before McDonald's team quickly made "The Pit" its home fortress. The versatile Hanson was named to the Class L All-State team the next season, when Holy Cross improved to 13-7. "Tom Amodeo and Ray White were team leaders that year, as the squad gained in experience and confidence," recalls Samuelson.

Hanson repeated as an All-Stater the following season, when Holy Cross, led by a battle-hardened group of seniors, completed an undefeated (20-0) regular season to claim the 1973 Naugatuck Valley League title in its first season as league member.

"By that year, our senior season, we had a fanatical student fan base and every home game was a sellout," says Samuelson. "If you didn't have your ticket for a Friday night game by mid-week, you were not getting into the gym."

A come-from-behind win over Naugatuck and a victory over Hartford Public – the top-ranked team in Connecticut at the time – were the most memorable games that season for Samuelson. "The win over Hartford Public marked the first time Holy Cross gained recognition among Connecticut's top teams," notes Samuelson. "Tony was his usual unstoppable self that night, and Jim Albon had an outstanding game as well."

An injury to point guard Duquette hampered the Crusaders' quest for a state title that season, but the foundation had been set for the young program to grow into a perennial league and state power.

Having taken over the fledgling program at age 24, McDonald's organized approach instilled a structure and discipline that would lead to six NVL titles and appearances in three state title games over his 18 years at the helm. The Crusaders captured the 1998 CIAC Class LL title in his last season as coach, before he moved on to serve as principal and then president at the school.

The program has certainly built further on those achievements, notes Samuelson, who succeeded McDonald as school president in 2015. "But he put Holy Cross on the map."

1973-74: Canady, Lee lead Wilby to titles

The 1973-74 season saw a fourth different city team in four years claim the Naugatuck Valley League crown, as Wilby relied on the strength of its frontcourt to compile a 13-1 record in the NVL (and an 18-4 overall mark).

Coach Jack Delaney's experienced frontline was headed by 6-6 Lou Canady, with fellow seniors, 6-4 Bob Gaston and 6-2 James Lee, adding support. Mike Stevenson, a 5-9 junior, added consistent scoring from the backcourt.

Canady averaged 15 points per game

Contributed / Wilby High School

Lou Canady of Wilby, lofting a hook shot over the Holy Cross defense, was named to the All-NVL team for a second time in 1973-74.

over the regular season and was named recipient of the Billy Finn award on Feb. 21, when the Wildcats defeated Crosby 71-57 to clinch the City Series. Sophomore Steve Johnson netted 27 points that night for the Bulldogs, a young team that finished just one win short of qualification for the CIAC tournament.

Holy Cross compiled a 12-8 record, having lost Tony Hanson and three other starters to graduation. The 1973-74 team was built around 6-7 junior Jim Abromaitis, who averaged 15 points a game and hit for 23 against both Sacred Heart and Watertown.

The Crusaders' opponent in the Class LL division playdown games was Notre Dame of West Haven, which had toppled Holy Cross in the last game of the regular season. But thanks to some pressure defense and 14 fourth-quarter points from freshman Clay Johnson, the 19th-ranked Crusaders claimed a 54-47 upset victory in the tourney contest.

Holy Cross stayed close to Trumbull in its next game, before the third-seeded Eagles used their size to wear down the Crusaders. All five Trumbull starters hit double figures in the 69-51 win, while Tom Claffey notched 14 points and Abromaitis added 11 in Holy Cross' final game of the season.

Led by 6-5 center Pop Baskins, Kennedy won eight of its last nine regular-season contests to earn a place in the CIAC tournament. And the streak continued in a playdown game of the Class L division, when the Eagles outscored Farmington 52-32 in the second half to advance by a 80-69 scoreline. Baskins shrugged off early foul trouble to score

27 points and Mel Cummings contributed 16 for 24th-rated Kennedy, which was 3-8 at one point of the season.

Marty Sweeney's Eagles next faced Rippowam of Stamford at Danbury. Kennedy fell behind once again, yet this time had no comeback as third-seeded Rippowam advanced with a 78-58 victory. Baskins (with 17 points) and Cummings (10) were the only double-figure scorers for Kennedy, which finished 12-10 on the season.

NVL champion Wilby earned the seventh seed in the Class L bracket, and opened with a 56-46 decision over Wilton. The Wildcats then played one of its best games of the season, as a strong shooting performance eliminated Maloney of Meriden. Junior guard Mike Stevenson netted 20 points to lead the way in 88-64 rout that improved Wilby's record to 17-3.

Stevenson and Lou Canady would foul out of the next game, a tense quarterfinal against second-seeded Bullard Havens of Bridgeport. Down by six points with four minutes remaining, Wilby rallied to take the lead on a Bob Gaston jumper in the final minute. Bullard-Havens' Joe Furman responded to knot the score, before a tip-in by Wilby's James Lee with eight seconds left gave the Waterbury team a dramatic win.

Wilby then faced a surprising Naugatuck squad, which it had beaten twice in the regular season, in the Class L semifinals. But the Greyhounds built a ten-point lead by halftime in the semi, and Wilby big man Canady picked up his fourth foul in the opening minute of the third period.

The Wildcats whittled the deficit down to two points late in the game, yet Naugatuck converted a number of free throws to claim a 74-66 win. John Palmer collected 26 points and 12 re-

Contributed / Wilby High School

James Lee of Wilby, recipient of the Lt. Jack Cullinan Award for sportsmanship in 1973-74.

bounds for the victors, while teammates Joe Healey and Gary Churchill also hit double figures. Canady topped Wilby with 17 points, James Lee scored 12 and Gaston netted 11 in the Wildcats' season-ending loss.

Lee was honored with the Lt. Jack Cullinan trophy (as city's top sportsman). The Doc McInerney award, presented annually to the top scholar-athlete among city teams, went to Bob Moffo of Sacred Heart.

Moffo and the Hearts failed to make postseason play but the 6-3 senior forward made history by scoring 39 points in his second-to-last game (a 91-69 win over Crosby) to surpass 1,000 points for his high school career.

31

Supporting their teams:
Cheerleaders from the 1970s

Contributed / Kaynor Tech High School

Contributed / Sacred Heart High School

Contributed / Wilby High School

Contributed / Crosby High School

Contributed / Kennedy High School

Contributed / Holy Cross High School

Contributed / Sacred Heart High School

Contributed / Crosby High School

Contributed / Wilby High School

Contributed / Kennedy High School

1974-75: Crosby stages a winning show to open 'The Palace'

Reprinted with permission of the Republican-American

Waterbury schools superintendent Michael F. Wallace tosses a ball up to Dave Wiggins of Crosby and John Kontout of Watertown as a ceremonial opening tip to begin the first game at the Crosby-Wallace gym on Dec. 6, 1974.

A number of teams seemed primed to make a run to dethrone defending league champion Wilby and capture the 1975 NVL title.

Holy Cross had lost only one starter from the previous year's team and featured one of the best big men in the state in 6-7 Jim Abromaitis. Kennedy also fielded a tall frontline with 6-6 Cecil Butler, 6-6 Bill Callahan and Waverly Robinson. And Naugatuck was coming off an appearance in the Class L final.

But the basketball gods seemed to time that season perfectly with the opening of Crosby High's new school and gymnasium, and the high-scoring Bulldogs rose to the top, with junior guard Steve Johnson and classmate Pete Anton leading the way.

The beautiful new Crosby-Wallace gymnasium, which would come to be known as the Crosby Palace, was officially opened for play on Dec. 6, 1974, when coach Bob Brown's Bulldogs raced past Watertown, 114-74. Six Crosby players reached double figures in scoring; 6-4 senior Dave Wiggins scored 20, with Johnson and senior Greg Stenson adding 18 each.

Crosby topped Holy Cross, 71-67, in its next outing to signal its intent on league supremacy. Johnson then paced the team to comfortable wins over Torrington and Naugatuck, before the Bulldogs set a city scoring record in a 125-71 rout of West Haven (with Anton netting a career-high 26 points).

The non-league victory was one of four times that Crosby topped the centu-

34

ry mark in a season when they were held below 70 points on just three occasions during the regular season.

One of those times was a 70-62 loss to Holy Cross, but the Bulldogs responded by winning their last four league games to finish with a12-2 NVL record (17-2 overall).

Johnson scored his team's first 13 points of the game and finished with 34 points in a key late-season win over Naugatuck. Two games later, Anton hit 12 of 13 field goals as Crosby topped Wilby, 82-63, on the final night of the regular season to clinch the city championship and celebrate an NVL title on its new home floor.

Seeded sixth in a competitive Class L state tournament bracket, Crosby opened against a tough Bassick team from Bridgeport. The back-and-forth affair culminated with the teams trading hoops in the fourth quarter.

Baskets by Johnson and Horace "Piggy" Williams each put the Bulldogs up by two points in the final minute before Bassick responded with hoops to tie the score. A 12-footer at the buzzer by Calvin Walker gave Bassick the 81-79 victory, seemingly ending Crosby's season.

But the CIAC determined days later that Bassick had used an ineligible player in the game, and Crosby won a protest to be placed back into the tournament.

Coach Bob Brown's squad cruised past Shelton, 93-77, in the next round to advance to a quarterfinal meeting with a team from Warren Harding of Bridgeport that featured Aldo Samuel and future NBA player Wes Matthews.

Crosby held its own in the first half before the third-seeded Presidents opened a double-digit lead in the third period. The Bulldogs rallied to trim the deficit down to two points, but were eventually eliminated, 70-66.

Steve Johnson scored 13 points in the loss; the total put the junior guard over 1,000 points for his career. Dave Wiggins also scored 13, with fellow senior Joe Gorman adding 12 for Crosby.

Holy Cross was also ousted by a Bridgeport school in the state tournament, after prevailing in its opener. Abromaitis notched 23 points and 15 rebounds, Mark Serafin scored 13 points and sophomore Clay Johnson, younger brother of Crosby's Steve, added 12 in an 85-64 win over Wethersfield in the

Contributed / Crosby High School

Guard Steve Johnson lays in two points for Crosby during the Bulldogs' league championship season.

1974-75 NVL champion Crosby Bulldogs

Crusaders' Class LL opener. But third-seeded Bridgeport Central proved too much for Holy Cross in the next round, ending the Crusaders' 1974-75 campaign.

Kaynor Tech, a city school but not a member of the Naugatuck Valley League, compiled a 16-2 record in the regular season, earning a place in the Class M tournament. Coach Dick Ierardi's Panthers lost a first-round battle with Northwest Catholic, 58-56; Pete Lieber scored 19 points and Irving Sands contributed 13 in the defeat.

Abromaitis, named to the *New Haven Register*'s All-State team in Class LL, was honored with the Billy Finn Award as top senior in Waterbury, on the final night of regular-season games. Crosby's Joe Gorman received the Doc McInerney Award as the top scholar-athlete in the city and guard Don Booker of Sacred Heart was selected for the Jack Cullinan award, given each year for sportsmanship.

Crosby's Johnson and Anton helmed the 1975 All-NVL team, joined by Abromaitis of Holy Cross, Naugatuck's Gary Churchill and Mike Stevenson of Wilby.

Jim Abromaitis of Holy Cross, the Billy Finn Award as top senior in Waterbury for 1974-75, was named to the New Haven Register's All-State team in Class LL.

Looking Back: Crosby's Pete Anton

"I had one of those rare 'in the zone' nights, going 12 for 13. It felt like I couldn't miss," remembers Pete Anton in describing his performance in Crosby's 82-63 victory over Wilby that clinched the city championship and NVL title for the 1974-75 season.

The setting that night made the Bull-dogs' title-clincher even more special. An overflow crowd was on hand for the team's final regular-season home game in their first season in their new gym dubbed the "Crosby Palace" (after playing most games at Kennedy High in previous seasons).

Anton and his teammates didn't disappoint the home fans, cruising past the visiting Wildcats to give coach Bob Brown the first of his two league titles during his decade at the helm of the Old Ivy team.

"The new school and gym were great. The team really welcomed our earlier practice time of 2:00 p.m. (versus 4:00 p.m the previous year at Kennedy)" recalls Anton. "We finally had our own home court to defend and I think the entire school embraced that challenge from the start of the 1974-75 season.

"The 'Palace' and our fans became our sixth man, making visiting teams feel very uncomfortable. It was just great having our own home court advantage for the first time," continues Anton, who would be named an All-City performer for two seasons and All-NVL forward in 1974-75.

He considers the win over Wilby among the most memorable games in his scholastic career. Others include hitting the game-winning shot in the closing seconds of a win over Sacred Heart during his sophomore season in 1974, and the 1976 CIAC Class L semifinal at the New Haven Coliseum.

"That one in 1976 (a loss to Warren Harding of Bridgeport) was memorable only because it was so disappointing to end our season that way. Harding had a very good team but we all knew, at our best, we could have won that game.

"Stevie (Johnson, the team's leading scorer) was double teamed most of the game," remembers Anton. "Steve Zaksewicz played great. But collectively we did not get the job done."

Crosby led by five points at the half. But Harding's Wes Matthews (who went on to play in the NBA) and Mike McKay (a future star at UConn) sparked a second-half surge to rally the Bridgeport team, which had also knocked Crosby out of the state tourney a year earlier.

"Looking back, I think our best chance to win it all was in 1974-75," says Anton. "We had speed, size and depth. We could press full court the entire game if needed. We were solid on both ends of the court."

That year, the Bulldogs had "a solid eight-man rotation with me, Stevie (Johnson), Horace Williams, Dave Wiggins, Greg Stenson, Joe Gorman, Steve Zaksewicz and Dave Steck," says Anton. "We won both city and NVL Championships and should have gone further in the tournament. Sadly, we did not play our best ball on the biggest stage."

A knee injury sustained in a Pearl Street summer basketball league game in 1975 lingered into Anton's senior season, when he and star guard Johnson returned to lead the Bulldogs. "We were still a very good team that senior year, but not nearly as deep or powerful as the previous one," says Anton, who was honored with the Lt. Jack Cullinan award for sportsmanship among city seniors.

In mentioning the rivalries with city schools during his scholastic career, Anton recalls that "we really never took any team

Crosby junior Pete Anton scores two of his 24 points in the Bulldogs' 82-63 win over Wilby before a packed house at the Crosby Palace. The victory clinched the Naugatuck Valley League title for the 1974-75 season.

for granted … as there were so many good solid players throughout the league.

"Players from around the NVL that most made an impression on me included, of course, the guys from Holy Cross: Jim Abromaitis, Clay Johnson, and Bob Allen," says Anton. "Mike Stevenson, Gary Lee and Bill Ramonas at Wilby were tough to handle. Pop Baskins at Kennedy was dominant on and around the boards. And Bob Moffo, Don Booker and Dave Rossi at Sacred Heart gave us fits."

Comparing the different eras of basketball in the city and the league, Anton notes that "the NVL was a much different game in the 1970s than it is now. It would be interesting to see how today's offensive style would fare against our '70s defense," he ponders.

"I know I would have loved the three-point line," he adds. "Though I can't say the same for those oversized baggy shorts."

Thinking back on the days of shorter shorts, Anton says "most of my high school memories have become hazy. However, the one memory that will always be clear in my mind is that Coach Brown and Coach Augelli did an amazing job getting the very most out of a skinny kid from the East End of Waterbury."

After high school, Anton attended Post Junior College for two years before heading to Eckerd College in St. Petersburg, Fla. "I came back to Connecticut in 1980 and worked with my father in construction for a year before taking a position at the Waterbury Republican-American in distribution/circulation."

He left the Republican-American in 1983 and spent the next 35 years doing similar work throughout Connecticut and Massachusetts. "I am an avid golfer now, so a move south is in my near future. Go Bulldogs," says Anton.

1975-76: Crusaders and Bulldogs remain on top; Kaynor sets mark

A trio of teams would garner most of the city's attention during the 1975-76 season, with Crosby and Holy Cross again battling it out for NVL honors and Kaynor Tech fashioning a 17-0 regular season record before falling to a city opponent in state tournament play.

Kaynor, the city's technical school, featured a number of returning players from a team that went 16-2 and made the state tournament the previous year, led by seniors Hank Spellman and Bob Kundrotas and junior guard Chris White.

The Panthers had few close contests throughout the campaign before big man Kundrotas broke his hand late in the season. His Kaynor teammates took on more of the scoring and rebounding duties while he was out, and Kaynor claimed three wins in the final week to finish off the perfect regular season for the first time in school history.

White and Spellman combined for 42 points in a 87-53 rout of Whitney Tech, and White netted 29 in a 75-69 win over Nonnewaug in the final game of the season. Kaynor had control of the game but Nonnewaug rallied to claim a 57-53 lead in the final period. Sophomore Mark Lefky, who scored 53 in three contests in the absence of Kundrotas, sparked a late surge to rally the Panthers, who earned the top seed in the

Chris White of Kaynor Tech.

CIAC Class L tournament.

Crosby was selected as the eighth seed in the Class L bracket, after winning 17 of 18 games following an 0-2 start to the season.

The Bulldogs' season opener, against New Haven's Lee High, was billed as a contest between two of Connecticut's top teams and didn't disappoint. Lee's 6-7 center Sly Williams – who would be named an All-American by some publications – scored 31 points to lead the New Haven school to a come-from-behind 76-73 victory.

Crosby had control for most of the game and led 37-29 at halftime, with Steve Johnson netting 16 points. The Bulldogs led until Williams hit a jumper halfway through the fourth period to put Lee up for good. Johnson finished with 29 points and Pete Anton added 16 for Crosby.

The defending NVL champion Bulldogs also dropped their next game, 69-61 to Holy Cross, conceding the early lead in the league race to their city rivals. Senior co-captain Bob Allen scored 23 points for the Crusaders, whose defense limited Crosby's chances in the impressive road win. Holy Cross junior Clay Johnson registered 13 points and 13 rebounds in the battle against older brother Steve, who scored 15 points for the Bulldogs.

Holy Cross remained the frontrunner

Crosby and Kaynor Tech tip off the 1976 Class L tournament quarterfinal at Kennedy High.

for the NVL title throughout the season, and again got the better of Crosby in the return matchup. Clay Johnson registered 26 points and 21 rebounds while Allen also scored 26 in the game that gave Tim McDonald's Crusaders a two-game lead over Crosby at the top of the NVL standings.

With Pete Shambreskis and Mark Giorgio adding support for Allen and Johnson, Holy Cross finished the NVL season with a 14-0 mark (and 15-4 overall record), earning the school its second league title and a berth in the Class LL tourney.

The Crusaders opened state play against Hartford Public, a team it had split games with during the regular season. The third meeting was a dramatic affair that extended into overtime after Holy Cross rallied from 11 points down in the final minutes to force the extra session.

Shambreskis, who would finish with 14 points, and Duncan Richardson (13 points) led the Crusaders' late charge, with Richardson's jumper beating the buzzer to tie the score.

But Public scored the first five points of overtime and held on for a 71-68 victory. Allen's 16 points and Johnson's 15 were tops for Holy Cross, which ended its season with a 15-5 record.

In a Class L opener, Crosby's pressure defense was too much for Waterford to handle in a 90-58 rout. Steve Johnson collected 34 points, nine rebounds and seven assists and Pete Anton, Steve Zaksewicz and Horace "Piggy" Williams also reached double figures in the playdown round win.

In the next round, Johnson notched a career-high 37 points and the 6-5 Zaksewicz added 19 as Crosby rolled past East Catholic, 86-70, to set up a quarterfinal contest against Kaynor Tech.

Bob Kundrotas had returned to action in Kaynor's 52-50 win over Darien, hitting two key hoops late in the Panthers' first-round victory.

The much-anticipated tournament game between city schools went Crosby's way, 77-60, with some hot shooting staking the Bulldogs to a 44-31 halftime lead in the game played at Kennedy High. Johnson ended with 28 points – to give him 99 points in three tournament games – while Williams and Zaksewicz contributed 14 each as Crosby claimed its 20th win of the season.

Bob Murphy scored 20 points for Kaynor, whose season ended at 18-1 at the hands of a Bulldog team gaining momentum in the postseason.

Crosby's 1975-76 season would end in similar fashion to the previous year's campaign — in a loss to the same opponent, Warren Harding, on the same day of the calendar, March 8. This time it was one round further in the state tournament — the Class L semifinals — at the New Haven Coliseum.

The Bulldogs started well enough on the big stage of the Coliseum, as Bob Brown's squad claimed a 35-30 advantage at the half. But Harding produced a 12-0 scoring run during the third period to take control.

Harding's Mike McKay, a 6-4 sophomore, led all scorers with 24 points and Wes Matthews tossed in 15 as the Bridgeport school held on for a 69-59 win. Zaksewicz finished with 20 points while Anton and Williams scored 13

each for Crosby.

Steve Johnson, who scored just eight points in the loss, ended his career as his school's and the city's all-time scoring leader with 1,494 points. He was named as a first-team All-State selection for Class L by the New Haven Register, alongside future NBA players Wes Matthews of Warren Harding and Mike Gminski of Masuk. (Bob Dulin of Foran and Al Carfaro of East Haven also made the Class L first team.)

Johnson and teammate Anton were named to the All-City team, joined by Clay Johnson and Bob Allen of Holy Cross and Sacred Heart's Craig Kazlauskas. Three of that group were honored with the city's senior awards — Steve Johnson claimed the Billy Finn award as the outstanding senior player in Waterbury, Anton earned the Lt. Jack Cullinan Award as top sportsman, and Allen was honored as top scholar-athlete with the Doc McInerney Award.

Kaynor Tech's Chris White and Bob Kundrotas were named second-team All-City selections. Crosby's Piggy Williams, Kennedy's George Washington and Bill Ramonas of Wilby joined the Kaynor pair on the second unit.

The brothers Johnson and Allen were named to the all-NVL team along with Frank Russo of Torrington and Bob Stauffer of Naugatuck.

Reprinted with permission of the Republican-American

Clay Johnson led Holy Cross to a 14-0 regular-season mark in the NVL in 1976-77, and was named to the All-City and All-NVL teams.

Blizzard conditions couldn't stop Johnson from setting city's scoring record

Mother Nature has a way of wreaking havoc on winter sports schedules in the Northeast, and high school basketball in Waterbury is no exception.

I can recall that the Naugatuck Valley League tried a few times in the early 1990s to build a league tournament onto the end of its schedule. Yet each time, a plethora of snow-related cancellations of regular-season games extended those seasons so long that the postseason tourneys had to be nixed each occasion.

I remember the showdown for the 1995 NVL title between Holy Cross and Ansonia being postponed by a storm. I also recall the 1998 Class L final being moved from a Saturday to Monday because of snow, and thus waiting two days longer to witness Crosby's first-ever state title.

I can remember being so upset as a Crosby junior to see it start snowing around lunchtime one day, threatening that night's huge Crosby-Holy Cross matchup for the 1981-82 NVL title. But a classmate in my 6th-period Trigonometry class had a wacky idea to counter the storm – we'd close the window blinds for the duration of the math period, he'd utter some magic words once the bell sounded to end the period, and we'd then lift the blinds to see that the snow had stopped for good. To our amazement, Mike Floridia's antics somehow did the trick, and the Bulldogs went on to win the first Naugatuck Valley league title during Nick Augelli's career as head coach that evening.

Another wild snow story centering around Crosby basketball occurred on a January night in 1976, when the Bulldogs were slated to host Weaver High of Hartford at The Palace.

The Bulldogs' star guard Steve Johnson had finished the previous game three points shy of becoming the city's all-time leading scorer, and plans were in place for an in-game presentation recognizing Johnson's accomplishment once he surpassed the mark of 1,204 points set by Wilby's Bobby Brown in 1962.

But the historic bucket, the ceremony and a dramatic battle between two of the state's top teams almost never came to be that evening, thanks to a major snowstorm and an erroneous radio report that the game was cancelled.

Snow began to fall in the area by late afternoon that day, with the rate of snowfall growing by the hour. A number of Crosby players who heard of the "postponement" by radio were surprised by phone calls from Coach Bob Brown that the game was still on, and scrambled to find a ride to the school.

But 15 minutes before the 8:00 tipoff, four of Crosby's regular starters had not yet arrived at the gym. Johnson, traveling with reserve Dwight Dildy, had gotten stuck in the snow on Meriden Road on the way there. "I didn't think we'd get to the game, but Piggy (Horace Williams) came by and picked us up," Johnson would tell the *Republican*'s Tom Talarico after the game.

Williams, Johnson's backcourt mate, was settled in at home for the night until hearing from his coach around 7:00 p.m. He gathered his gear and headed to Crosby, making his first "assist" of the night before the game even started by rescuing stranded teammates.

Crosby center Steve Zaksewicz arrived at Crosby at 7:50, around the same time Williams' car pulled into the school's parking lot. Another starter, Toby Harrison, didn't show until after the game had started – having been at a friend's house while thinking the game had been called off.

Despite the scrambling and limited pre-game warmup, Johnson and Crosby produced one of their best halves of the season against a 9-1 Weaver team led by guard George Davis and 6-8 Rick Mahorn, a future NBA player.

Sparked by the play of senior Pete Anton – who was inserted into the lineup after originally planning to sit out the game to nurse an injury – the Bulldogs held a 49-47 lead at halftime, to the delight of around 1,000 spectators who braved the storm to witness history.

That record-breaking moment came midway through the first period, when Johnson hit a baseline jumper to give him four points for the game and 1,205 for his scholastic career. A brief stoppage at that point saw Johnson presented with the game ball, along with a trophy by the Crosby Alumni Association.

With blizzard conditions raging outside, the battle between two of the state's top teams continued to entertain into the second half. Crosby's lead reached double figures at one point in the third period, only for the visiting Beavers to cut the deficit to three points entering the final quarter.

Weaver took the lead on a number of occasions in the fourth period. But the host Bulldogs retained their poise, and a Piggy Williams basket with a minute-and-a-half remaining gave Crosby the lead for good.

Williams – who played a major role for his team before the game – then had the chance to secure the role of hero on the court when headed to the free throw line with 23 seconds left. With Crosby leading, 83-82, he calmly sank both foul shots to provide a three-point lead, and the Bulldogs held on for an 85-84 victory to raise their record on the season to 9-2.

Five players reached double figures for Crosby, led by Anton's 18 points and 15

each from Johnson and Harrison. Williams added 12 points, while Harrison and Zaksewicz did their part on the backboards by combining for 25 rebounds.

Davis was the game's high scorer with 19 points and Mahorn added 16 for Weaver, which would advance all the way to the Class LL final that season before falling to Lee of New Haven.

"I was a little nervous after missing my first shot of the night," Johnson told the *Republican*'s Talarico after the game. "Besides breaking the record, this was one of the greatest wins I've ever played in. You can't believe how much we wanted to win this game."

Johnson would end his scholastic career with 1,494 points. While that total has since been topped by a number of players, I'd wager no one set a new city record under such extraordinary circumstances.

Contributed /Crosby High School

Rick Mahorn of Hartford Weaver looks on as Crosby's Steve Johnson releases the jumper that gave him 1,205 career points, breaking the city's all-time scoring record.

1976-77: Holy Cross repeats as league champions

Holy Cross became the first school to repeat as Naugatuck Valley League champion in six years, winning all 14 league games to claim the 1976-77 title – and complete a 20-0 regular-season record for the second time (the first coming in the 1973-74 campaign).

"Four years ago it was almost expected of us," coach Tim McDonald told reporters after win number 20. "But this team had to work hard to complete an undefeated season."

The 1976-77 Crusaders' knack for prevailing in close contests began with a 72-64 overtime win over Crosby in their league opener. Senior Clay Johnson scored 21 points and Holy Cross rallied from seven points behind midway through the third period to win.

That was followed by a 53-52 decision over Sacred Heart and a 60-58 road win at East Catholic, the first two of nine victories by four points or less by Holy Cross over the course of the season. Others included a one-point win at Ansonia, which would go on to finish second in the NVL standings, and a 59-57 victory over Wilby – with Johnson completing a three-point play in the final minute to secure the win for the Crusaders.

Senior co-captain Mark Giorgio netted 10 points in that game and followed that up with a 14-point effort in the Crusaders' come-from behind victory at Hartford Public. The hosts had a double-digit lead in the first half before Holy Cross fought back behind the 6-3 Johnson and sophomore Todd Hart, who

also finished with 14 points.

The 14 NVL wins extended the Crusaders' league streak to 31 consecutive games. Coincidentally, that same number of wins – 31 – represented a run of regular-season victories compiled by Kaynor Tech before the Panthers lost to city foe Sacred Heart in an early-season contest.

Six-foot-six senior center Ken Kazlauskas notched 15 points and 9 rebounds in that 64-50 victory for Sacred Heart, who went on to finish with a 12-8 overall record to qualify for the state tournament after missing out on postseason play the previous three seasons.

Seeded eighth in the CIAC Class M bracket, Sacred Heart held off Brookfield, 61-54, in the first round. Kazlauskas scored 26 points and fellow senior Pete Duglenski recorded a three-point play and a key assist in the closing minutes to seal the win.

The Hearts then faced top-seeded Middletown and future UConn star Corny Thompson in the quarterfinals. Kazlauskas was called for two fouls in the first minute and Sacred Heart never got into gear, falling 74-50 to Middletown, who would go on to claim a second consecutive Class M crown.

The LL division featured two Waterbury schools in top-seeded Holy Cross and tenth-ranked Crosby. The Bulldogs, who had moved up from Class L, had a halftime lead over Stamford Westhill before losing, 82-72, in the first round. Bob Hardison and Toby Harrison, the lone returning starter from the previous

The 1976-77 All-City team included, from left, Ken Kazlauskas of Sacred Heart, Crosby's Toby Harrison, Chris White of Kaynor Tech, Clay Johnson of Holy Cross and Kennedy's George Washington.

year, paced Crosby, which finished 14-7 for the season.

Top seed Holy Cross endured yet another close call in its Class LL opener, needing a three-point play by 6-5 Jim Shaw in the closing seconds to force overtime against Simsbury. Shaw and Duncan Richardson then scored key hoops in the extra session as the Crusaders escaped with a 49-47 win.

Next up was familiar foe Hartford Public, a team Holy Cross had defeated in the regular season and the school that had knocked the Crusaders out of the state tournament the previous year.

Holy Cross took an early lead in the Class L quarterfinal played at Bristol Central, but a 16-2 run by Hartford Public gave the Owls a 36-25 advantage at halftime. The duo of Ken Smith and Charles Jernigan continued their hot shooting in the second half and combined for 49 points on the night to lead Public to a 74-67 decision.

Mark Giorgio scored 17 points and Clay Johnson netted 14 as Holy Cross was eliminated by the same school on the same floor as Tim McDonald's

1975-76 squad.

Johnson, who started 85 times and missed only one game in four seasons at Holy Cross, finished his high school career with 1,183 points, second only to Tony Hanson's 1,222 points in the school's history to that point.

He was named the 1977 recipient of the Billy Finn Award as the outstanding senior player in the city. His Holy Cross teammate Bob Delaney, son of Wilby coach Jack Delaney, earned the Doc McInerney Award as the top scholar-athlete among city seniors. And the Lt. Jack Cullinan Award for sportsmanship was shared by George Washington of Kennedy and Kaynor Tech's Chris White, who also surpassed the 1,000-point scoring plateau during his senior season.

Johnson and White, each named as All-State selections by the New Haven Register, headed the All-City team for 1976-77. They were joined by Ken Kazlauskas of Sacred Heart, Kennedy's George Washington and Toby Harrison of Crosby, marking the first time in 33 years that the All-City team featured players from five different schools.

Brother vs. Brother: Sibling rivalries on city courts

There are several instances where pairs of brothers have played alongside each other on high school teams in Waterbury over the years. City hoop fans will remember Garnett and Garrett Petteway together on some of Kennedy's best teams, and Mustapha Heron and Raheem Solomon on state title squads at Sacred Heart, to name a couple of notable sibling partnerships.

But there have only been a few instances where brothers opposed each other in city and Naugatuck Valley League contests, with the most memorable being a pair of siblings facing off while starring for Holy Cross and Crosby in the mid-1970s.

Mention the "Brothers Johnson" to people, and some will recall the R&B group known for such hits as "Strawberry Letter 23" and "I'll Be Good to You" in the 1970s. But Waterbury had its own popular Brothers Johnson around that same time: Steve Johnson and Clay Johnson, entertaining city sports fans on a different type of stage.

The two faced each other six times over three seasons, with Clay's Holy Cross teams winning on four occasions in games against Steve's Crosby squads. The siblings each led their team to city and NVL titles and each topped 1,000 points in their scholastic careers.

Steve, who finished his senior season as Crosby's all-time leading scorer with 1,494 points, was named to the Class L All-State team in 1976 and went on to play at Wagner College.

Clay, who graduated one year after his brother, was a key member of two NVL title-winning teams at Holy Cross. He earned All-State honors in 1977 and went on to play for the University of Connecticut.

Two decades later, another set of brothers squared off on opposite sides of the Crosby-Holy Cross rivalry, when Robert Saunders led Bulldog teams against younger brother Edmund and the Crusaders. Rob would appear on an All-City team, while Edmund helped lead the Crusaders to a state title in 1995 and eventually finish as the school's all-time scoring leader.

The 1990s also saw Marvin and Jermel Rountree square off in city contests. In the 1996-97 season, Marvin's Sacred Heart team won a CIAC title while Jermel's Kennedy squad was also ranked among the top 15 teams in the state.

While those siblings certainly made their mark on the city's hoop history, Steve and Clay Johnson, together with younger brother Bruce – who starred at Holy Cross from 1978 to 1981 and also gained All-State status as a senior– have arguably remained as Waterbury's "first family" of basketball.

The 1976 All-City team featured brothers Clay and Steve Johnson.

1977-78: Crosby claims NVL crown; two new coaches join ranks

A pair of new coaches for city teams and a new state tournament format marked the changes for the 1977-78 high school basketball season in Connecticut.

The CIAC introduced a regional setup for the early rounds in each class, with the two teams that reached the final in each of four regions advancing to the quarterfinals for that class. This format, allowing the losers in region finals to remain in the tournament, would stay in place through the early 1980s.

Jack Taglia replaced Marty Sweeney as head coach at Kennedy High, after serving for two years as an assistant to Sweeney. And Bob Freeman assumed the helm at Wilby, taking over for the departed Jack Delaney.

Freeman inherited an experienced squad to ease the transition; Wilby's returning lettermen included 6-4 junior Dale Saunders along with Jay Seay, Bob Butler and Larry Garlington. The Wildcats fared well, winning 10 of their first 14 games before finishing 11-5 (10-5 in the NVL) and then advancing to the second round of the CIAC Class L tournament, where they lost to league foe Torrington.

Torrington was in contention for the NVL crown until the final week,

Reprinted with permission of the Republican-American

Sacred Heart coach John Gilmore, right, is joined by two new head coaches in the city prior to the 1977-78 season: Wilby's Bob Freeman, left and Jack Taglia of Kennedy.

when it dropped a 71-70 decision to Holy Cross after the Crusaders' Pete Rode sank a 20-footer with two seconds remaining. That result gave the league title to Crosby, which compiled a 13-3 NVL record.

The Bulldogs lost key player Charlie Montgomery to injury early in the year, but relied on Mark White's inside game and Johnny Kidd's floor leadership to give coach Bob Brown a second league championship during his tenure.

The 6-5 White, who would be named winner of the Billy Finn award that season, scored in double figures in all but two games. He notched 16 points and 13 rebounds in an early-season 77-66 win over Holy Cross that ended the Crusaders 31-game winning streak in league play, and recorded 18 points and 27 rebounds in Crosby's 69-62 victory over Sacred Heart later in the campaign.

But the Hearts would gain some revenge in the postseason, upsetting Crosby 74-62 in a Class L opener within the state's new regional setup. Duane Clements netted 25 points and Vin De-Vico added 18 points and 11 rebounds as the Sacred Heart held on for the Class L victory.

Involved in a tight contest with North Haven in the next round, the Hearts scored six straight points in the final minute to take a one-point lead. But the late surge did not result in victory, as a Vic Urbanski jumper fell through the net at the buzzer to give North Haven a 63-62 win that ended Sacred Heart's season at 13-9.

Devico, who scored 16 points in the tourney loss, was the season's recipient of the Jack Cullinan Award as the senior who displayed the most sportsmanship. Crosby's Mark Wawer joined teammate White among senior award winners as

he was presented with the Doc McInerney Award as top scholar-athlete among city seniors.

Crosby's White and Kidd were named to the all-NVL team, along with Torrington's Ray Amejko, JoJo Shortell of Ansonia and Holy Cross junior Spencer Harrison, who led the league in scoring with a 20.8 average.

White and Harrison were joined on the All-City squad by Jay Seay of Wilby, Greg Yates of Sacred Heart and Kennedy's Willie Daniels.

Contributed /Crosby High School

Crosby's Mark White received the Billy Finn Award as the outstanding senior player in the city for the 1977-78 season.

Looking Back: Coach Bob Brown

"Crosby's 1977-78 Naugatuck Valley League title came as a bit of a surprise for Bob Brown – the Bulldogs' coach from the 1968-69 through 1978-79 seasons – in comparison to the squads he guided throughout his decade at the helm.

"In 1977-78 we had a new group of players assuming key roles, led by Mark White, Johnny Kidd, Mark Wawer and Jeff Mitchell," says Brown. "It was a different scenario from the 1974-75 championship team, which was deep and experienced and loaded with great players."

The 1977-78 Bulldogs had also lost Charlie Montgomery to injury, "yet rallied behind White and Kidd to finish atop the NVL standings,' recalls Brown. "Late in the season, Johnny Kidd completed a drive in the final five seconds for a win that tied us for the lead with Holy Cross with one NVL game left to play.

"We won our next game and Holy Cross lost theirs, so we won the league and I was the most surprised coach in the league," says Brown, whose team had defeated the Crusaders earlier in the season to break a 31-game league win streak by the Crusaders.

"The Holy Cross game was always for bragging rights among the city high schools," remembers Brown. "Timmy McDonald, a great coach, was always prepared for us. I always said if we could win just one game a year it would be one of the Holy Cross games. All those games were classics and most of the times they had our number."

Playing its main rivals on a true home court proved beneficial for the Bulldogs, after the school moved from its downtown site to a new complex on Pierpont Road in September of 1974.

"Prior to that season, we used to practice at Wilby and Kennedy gyms, but it was not a good situation as we had to squeeze in time between other schools," notes Brown. "Finally, in 1974, the 'Palace' opened. We could practice right after school ended on our own court, and the system we worked on for years came to life."

Bob Brown

The Bulldogs claimed a first NVL title for Brown in that initial season in their new home, which was built to hold over 2,500 sitting fans and began sharing duties with Kennedy as a neutral site for various city contests.

"Once Dr. Wallace, Superintendent of Schools, threw up the ceremonial opening tip to start the first game of that season, we were off and running," says Brown. "With our talent and depth, we were able to play a running and pressing style throughout games to outlast opponents."

Juniors Steve Johnson, Pete Anton and Piggy Williams combined with seniors Dave Wiggins, Joe Gorman and Greg Stenson to lead the 1974-75 Bulldogs to city and league honors.

Crosby and Holy Cross would remain at the top and trade NVL titles over Brown's final few seasons on the bench. "But all the city teams, at one time or another during my time as coach, were great," says Brown – who selected the following group as the top players in the city over that time: "Sacred Heart's Gary Franks, Johnny Booker of Kennedy, Kaynor Tech's Chris White, Tony Hanson of Holy Cross, Wilby's Larry Chapman ... and the very best, Stevie Johnson of Crosby!"

1978-79: Harrison leads Holy Cross to title; Wilby moves to new home

The changes at Wilby High School in the late 1970s continued into the 1978-79 season. One year after Bob Freeman took over as coach for the boys basketball team, the school moved into a new complex in the North End of Waterbury.

Wilby's expansive new gym was dedicated prior to the team's home opener on December 16, 1978, when the Wildcats cruised past visiting Ansonia, 79-48. Steve Sawyer scored 20 points while Jay Seay and Archie Williams netted 11 apiece in the rout, the first win of a season that would see Wilby challenge for city and league crowns.

Seay's 23 points paced the Wildcats to a 79-73 win over defending NVL champion Crosby, as Wilby served notice that it was a contender for the league title with a string of early wins.

But the streak came to an end against Holy Cross in a mid-season battle that paired two teams sporting 7-0 league records. The Crusaders scored 16 of the game's final 21 points to rally for a 68-63 road win and secure first place in the NVL standings.

Spencer Harrison emerged as Holy Cross' go-to scorer in the 1978-79 season, flirting with a 30-point scoring average for much of the season – highlighted by a 36-point effort in a 96-89 overtime win at Crosby and a school-record 39 points against Torrington.

Fellow senior Todd Hart was a strong inside presence for Holy Cross, which also featured a talented pair of sophomore guards in John Burrus and Bruce Johnson.

The Crusaders maintained their lead at the top of the league and held off Wilby, 66-64, in the final week of the season to clinch the NVL title. Harrison was held to 15 points but Hart scored 12 and Ken Clisham added 14 off the bench for Holy Cross.

With the league crown in hand, the Crusaders claimed top seed in the league's new postseason tournament, which featured the top four teams in the regular-season standings. Holy Cross

Contributed /Holy Cross High School

Spencer Harrison averaged 29.6 points per game in his senior season, finishing his scholastic career as the all-time scoring leader at Holy Cross.

captured that as well, topping Sacred Heart before defeating Wilby in the final, 60-55, with sophomores Burrus and Johnson making key hoops late in the game.

Five teams from Waterbury qualified for the CIAC tournament. Holy Cross earned the No. 3 overall ranking in Class L, Crosby and Kaynor Tech claimed places in Class L, and Wilby was matched against Sacred Heart in the first round of the Class M Region III bracket.

The Hearts and Wildcats had split two regular-season matchups, and the postseason affair was a close contest throughout. A Steve Sawyer basket broke a 60-60 tie and put Wilby up for good, and the Wildcats held on for a 71-64 win. Jay Seay was the game's high scorer with 17 points while Barry Smith netted 16 for Wilby. Jess McIntosh scored 16 and Duane Clements added 14 for Sacred Heart, whose season ended at 16-7.

Wilby would be eliminated in the next round, falling 88-74 to St. Thomas Aquinas of New Britain and star guard, Rod Foster, who scored 32 points. Seay and Archie Williams, Wilby's senior co-captains, led the team in scoring as the Wildcats finished 16-7.

Like Wilby, Crosby was eliminated from state tournament play in the second round. The Bulldogs ousted Guilford, 63-59 in its Class L opener. Trailing with six minutes remaining, Dave Bryant and Mike Williams contributed four points each down the stretch to lead the Crosby comeback.

The Bulldogs then faced Cheshire, which had beaten Kaynor Tech of Waterbury in the first round and featured a frontline that included 6-9 Pete DeBisschop. Crosby's Williams scored a last-minute bucket to send the game into overtime before Cheshire prevailed, 67-66. DeBisschop netted 19 points while Crosby's Ron Maness scored a game-high 20 in Bob Brown's final game in charge as the Bulldogs' coach.

Holy Cross cruised past its first two opponents — West Hartford Hall and Simsbury — in Class LL play, before falling 77-58 to Northwest Catholic in the Region III final. Yet, with the new tournament format, the Crusaders still advanced to the LL quarterfinals, where they were matched against Hartford Public.

Contributed /Holy Cross High School

1978-79 NVL champion Holy Cross Crusaders

The 1978-79 All-City team included, from left, Spencer Harrison and Todd Hart of Holy Cross, Jay Seay of Wilby, Greg Yates of Sacred Heart and Charlie Montgomery of Crosby.

The Hartford team surged to a 10-point lead in the first period, but a pair of 11-0 runs by Holy Cross proved decisive as the Crusaders claimed an 82-78 decision to advance to the state semifinals for the first time in school history. Spencer Harrison poured in 31 points to surpass Tony Hanson's point total and become the Crusaders' all-time scoring leader.

Harrison would equal his single-game record of 39 points in the semifinal, which would turn out to be his final game in a Holy Cross uniform, as the Crusaders were eliminated by Wilbur Cross of New Haven, 97-95, in double overtime. Sophomore guards Bruce Johnson and John Burrus also reached double figures for Holy Cross, which ended the season with its most victories ever, at 23-4.

The 6-foot Harrison, who finished the season with a 29.6-point scoring average and was selected to the Class LL All-State squad, was named recipient of the Billy Finn Award as top senior in the city. The Jack Cullinan Award for sportsmanship went to Mark Butler of Sacred Heart, and Fred Keefe, teammate of Butler, was selected for the Doc McInerney Award as top scholar-athlete among city seniors.

The Holy Cross duo of Harrison and Todd Hart were joined on the All-City team by Jay Seay of Wilby, Crosby's Charlie Montgomery and Greg Yates of Sacred Heart.

Seay made mark at Wilby, Sacred Heart

The last of four city high school gymnasiums built over a 14-year period that helped advance Waterbury's hoop scene into the modern era, Wilby High's home court was part of an expansive complex housing the high school and North End Middle School that opened its doors to students for the 1978-79 school year.

In similar fashion to Crosby's move four years earlier from a older downtown location to a site on the outskirts of town, Wilby's basketball team nearly matched Crosby's title-wining success in its first season in a brand-spanking-new gymnasium. But the Wildcats finished second to Holy Cross in the Naugatuck Valley League standings, and then fell to the Crusaders in the final of the NVL postseason tournament, put into place for the first time that season.

"The student body was really excited about being the first group at the new Wilby High School complex," remembers Jay Seay, a senior co-captain for that year's basketball team. "And "having our own home court was certainly a boost for the team."

The Wildcats started the season with wins in their first seven games, which included a a 79-73 win over defending NVL champion Crosby. Seay paced the victors with 23 points in that victory, and netted 31 in a win over Kennedy, two of the memorable games during his senior season.

Another memorable contest "was at the new Wilby against Sacred Heart. It was a jam-packed gymnasium with an overflow crowd, and additional bleachers pulled out and placed under the baskets," recalls Seay.

Jay Seay

"The game went into overtime with the Wildcats earning a tough victory."

The 1978-79 Wilby team also claimed a win over Sacred Heart in the CIAC Class M tournament, before falling to state power St. Thomas Aquinas of New Britain to end its season at 16-7. Seay – named a first-team All-City performer – and his senior teammates had provided a solid foundation for the basketball program to build on as the first Wilby class to graduate in the new building.

Seay's mark on city hoops continued into modern times, culminating with serving as associate coach to Jon Carroll during Sacred Heart's streak of four consecutive state titles from 2014 to 2017.

Among the guidance and input Seay offered from the Hearts' bench, he made a point of delivering a specific inspirational message to the team prior to each game. And thanks to Marty Morra, Sacred Heart scorekeeper during that period who compiled season reviews for the Hearts, here are a select few of those messages:

■ "One Life, One Love, One Game," prior to the 2014 city jamboree

■ "Keep your eyes on the prize, not the obstacles," before a commanding victory over Wolcott in 2014

■ "If it is to be, it is We," prior to a game against rival Crosby in 2015

■ "Your dream is the reason you climb out of bed every morning and face the challenges of the world. Don't hide under the covers and miss your opportunity to achieve it," before the Hearts defeated nationally-ranked Christ the King of N.Y. in the HoopHall Classic in Springfield, Mass.

1979-80: Generali, Augelli find success in first year as coaches

City teams entered the 1979-80 season having to replace some key players lost to graduation, with no clear favorite for the Naugatuck Valley League title evident at the start of the campaign.

The time of transition was also marked by two schools promoting assistants into head coaching roles. Nick Augelli took over the position from Bob Brown at Crosby and Ed Generali assumed the post at Sacred Heart, following the retirement of John Gilmore.

The two new coaches who would become city legends faced each other in their first varsity games in charge; Crosby claimed a 74-62 home win over the Hearts as 6-2 senior Ron Maness led the way with 29 points for Augelli's Bulldogs.

Maness and 6-3 junior Dave Bryant took on the scoring load for Crosby's 1979-80 squad, which finished 12-4 in the league and 15-5 overall to earn berths in the NVL playoffs and CIAC tournament in Augelli's first season at the helm. The record included a 62-61 victory over city foe Holy Cross, when Maness hit two free throws with four seconds left in the game.

Holy Cross' lone returning starters were backcourt mates Bruce Johnson and John Burrus, yet the Crusaders put together another fine season, finishing second in the NVL with a 13-3 record (14-6 overall).

Losing Johnson to injury midway through the season, the Crusaders still went into the final week of games with a chance to share the league title, but Sacred Heart's 80-59 rout of Kennedy secured the championship for the Hearts. Senior guard Ken Sinclair scored 23 points in the title clincher, while junior Mark Redding contributed 17 points and six steals.

Sinclair emerged as a consistent scorer for a Sacred Heart team that had lost four double-digit scorers from the previous year. Daryl Parker and Bob Tehan, a pair of 6-3 big men, provided a frontcourt presence for Generali's Hearts, who turned what looked to be a rebuilding season into a championship campaign.

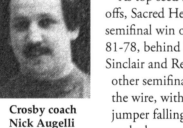

Crosby coach Nick Augelli

As top seed in the NVL playoffs, Sacred Heart rallied for a semifinal win over Torrington, 81-78, behind 18 points from Sinclair and Redding. The other semifinal went down to the wire, with Burrus' 15-foot jumper falling through the net as the buzzer sounded to give Holy Cross a 53-51 win over Crosby.

The Crusaders then avenged two regular-season losses to Sacred Heart by winning the NVL tourney final, 86-84. Burrus netted 21 points and center Craig Girch added 13 as Holy Cross prevailed in a game that was tied 18 times.

Holy Cross, one of six Waterbury teams qualifying for CIAC tournament play, fell to New Britain, 56-50, in its Class LL opener. Burrus and sophomore Carmen Giampetruzzi scored 12 points each for Tim McDonald's Crusaders.

Sacred Heart was paired against Wilby in a Class L Region I opener and held off the Wildcats, 77-70, with Sinclair and Redding top scorers on the night. But a hot-shooting East Catholic team eliminated the Hearts in the next round; Sinclair hit for 14 points and Parker scored 11 as Sacred Heart finished 18-6 in Generali's first season as head coach.

"I couldn't be happier with the season, though," Generali told the *Waterbury Republican* after the game. "We were looking for 10 wins, maybe a few more, and we ended up 18-6. I'm very happy with the way things went this year."

In the other game of a region semifinal double-header at Bristol Central that night, Crosby upset top-ranked and undefeated Maloney of Meriden, 60-59, on a jumper by Dave Bryant with 24 seconds remaining.

Contributed /Sacred Heart High School

Ken Sinclair of Sacred Heart received the Billy Finn Award as top senior player for the 1979-80 season.

Offsetting a 36-point performance by Maloney's 6-9 star Jay Murphy, the Bulldogs' balanced scoring effort included 18 from Maness, 15 from Bryant and 12 from freshman Deja Dennis.

Crosby continued its postseason run with an impressive 79-55 win over East Catholic to claim the Class L Region I championship. Dave Bryant notched 28 points and 13 rebounds while junior Bernie Ireland contributed 14 points for the Bulldogs.

A 41-37 decision over South Windsor followed, before Crosby was defeated by Bullard Havens of Bridgeport, 62-48, in the Class L semifinals. Maness netted 15 points and Bryant had 14 as the

Bulldogs' season ended at 20-7.

The Crosby duo were both named to the All-City and All-NVL teams. The NVL squad also included Sacred Heart's Sinclair, John Tuozzo of Torrington and Ansonia's Jeff Patulak.

Joining Maness and Bryant on the All-City team were Sinclair, John Burrus of Holy Cross and Kennedy's senior guard Tony Sica.

The Hearts' Sinclair received the Billy Finn Award as top senior player in the city. Malcolm Petteway of Crosby was presented with the Doc McInerney Award as outstanding scholar-athlete, and Crosby's Maness and Jim Corbett of Sacred Heart shared the Jack Cullinan Award for sportsmanship.

Selecting a 'High Five' for the 1970s

In wrapping up coverage of the first ten seasons for the book, I thought I would borrow an exercise used when I covered a couple of soccer World Cups while at espn.com – which involved selecting an All-Star team for each stage of those competitions (from group play, through the knockout rounds, at each tourney).

Instead of just choosing the best performers for each occasion, there were a couple of caveats included in the process: the group of selections had to fit within basic formations or lineups according to positions on the playing field, and only one player per team could be included.

Using a similar framework to select an all-star team for Waterbury high school basketball in the 1970s, here is one writer's attempt at a "High Five" for the decade.

■ With apologies to Jim Abromaitis, Spencer Harrison and Clay Johnson, the Holy Cross player featured on this team is Tony Hanson. He was one of only two players from Waterbury (along with Mustapha Heron) selected to the Connecticut Interscholastic Athletic Conference's All-Century Team – a list of 25 players announced in 2021, 100 years after the CIAC was first formed.

A two-time All-State selection, the 6-4 Hanson led the Crusaders to an undefeated regular season in 1972-73, the school's third year at the varsity level. The versatile performer was named Billy Finn Award winner his senior year and was the first player at Holy Cross to surpass 1,000 points for his scholastic career.

Contributed / Holy Cross High School

Tony Hanson of Holy Cross drives past a Wilby defender.

Hanson's stature grew further at UConn, scoring 1,990 career points and helping to lead the Huskies to a Sweet 16 NCAA appearance in his junior season. An original member of the Huskies of Honor (unveiled in 2007), Hanson enjoyed a long professional career in Europe, before becoming a coach and administrator in England.

He died in November 2018 at the age of 63, with former teammates and friends holding memorial events in Waterbury and Storrs.

■ Joining Hanson to complete the two forward positions on the All-70s team is another city native whose stature grew further in college. Bill Eason played just two impactful seasons at Kennedy High before going off to prep school and then Providence College – where he appeared in two NIT tourneys and two NCAAs in the late 1970s.

Eason was an All-City and All-NVL

pick as a 6-5 sophomore in 1971-72, when he averaged 22.8 points per game and helped to lead Kennedy to the school's first NVL title.

After serving the commonwealth of Massachusetts for 28 years as a Superior Court clerk magistrate – Eason also passed away unexpectedly, in September of 2017.

■ Crosby's Steve Johnson, the 1976 Billy Finn Award winner, fills the first of two guard spots on the All-'70s team. An outstanding shooter and defender, Johnson led a deep and talented Bulldog team to the NVL title in his junior season, the first of two seasons that he would be named to the All-NVL team.

While his first love was baseball, Johnson became a three-year starter for coach Bob Brown's Bulldogs, and finished his Crosby career as the city's all-time scoring leader – amassing 1,494 points without the benefit of the three-point shot.

After high school, Johnson played basketball at Wagner College before returning to the area. Sadly, he is the

Contributed / Wilby High School

Wilby's Lou Canady scores in the paint in a game at Kennedy High.

third member of this five-man squad to no longer be with us, having passed in November of 2013.

■ The other guard position goes to Gary Franks, who starred for two NVL-title winning teams at Sacred Heart. The 6-1 Franks averaged 29 points in his senior season, was a first-team All-State selection and one of the top players in New England in his graduating class of 1971.

After an outstanding career at Yale, Franks opted for the business world after an NBA tryout. He then served in local government before being elected to the U.S. House of Representatives in 1990, becoming the first Black Republican Congressman in nearly 60 years.

■ Lou Canady, the 1974 Billy Finn Award winner from Wilby High, completes the starting five for the All-'70s squad. The 6-6 center commanded the paint on both ends for the Wildcats, who claimed an NVL crown in 1973-74, his senior season.

A two-time All-NVL pick, Canady went to Eastern Connecticut State University. He became an addictions counselor, spending two decades at Connecticut Valley Hospital.

■ As a bonus, let's add a sixth man to the group, since every good team needs a solid bench.

Chris White of Kaynor Tech, a Class L All-State selection in 1976-77 who could play a number of positions on the court, fits the bill perfectly.

White surpassed 1,000 points for his scholastic career and was one of the key components to the Panthers' successes in a historic 1975-76 season, when Coach Dick Ierardi's team produced an undefeated regular season and reached the Class L quarterfinals.

The 1980s

Dewey Stinson of Holy Cross attempts to block a shot put up by Wilby's Dwayne Ellis in a game at the Wilby gym during the 1987-88 season.

1980-81: Crusaders return to top of the league, reach state final

Holy Cross enjoyed a successful 1980-81 season, reclaiming the NVL championship from Catholic school rival Sacred Heart, setting a school record for consecutive victories and reaching the CIAC Class LL championship game.

Senior guards Bruce Johnson and John Burrus guided coach Tim McDonald's Crusaders to a 16-0 record in Naugatuck Valley League contests after the team opened the season with a loss at Bishop McNamara in Maryland.

Johnson averaged 11 points a game while contributing an average of eight assists per outing, including two games with 13 assists and a season-high 15 assists in a win over Kennedy.

Backcourt mate Burrus scored at a 14 points-per-game clip, topped by 21 against Kennedy. The 5-11 senior netted 20 points and fueled a Holy Cross rally to defeat Sacred Heart, 54-50, in mid-January to solidify its place atop the NVL standings.

Cross cruised through its remaining league games to capture the school's fifth NVL title and earn the second overall seed in the CIAC Class LL tournament. Sacred Heart, which finished second in the NVL standings with a 13-3 league record, was paired against city foe Wilby in a Class L opener for the third season in a row. Crosby was also placed into Region IV of the Class L bracket while Kennedy claimed a berth in Region III of the Class M tourney.

Led by juniors Waddell Walton and John Maia, Kennedy opened the post-season with two impressive victories – an 83-42 rout of Cheney Tech and 101-74 defeat of Wolcott, with Maia collecting 36 points and 19 rebounds.

The Eagles then took perennial state power St. Thomas Aquinas of New Britain to three overtimes in the Class M Region III Final before falling 61-60. Despite the loss, Kennedy continued on to the quarterfinals as region finalists, but were eliminated by top-seeded Woodrow Wilson, 74-59.

In its Class L opener, Sacred Heart ousted Wilby by a 66-47 scoreline with Mark Redding's 19 points and Darryl Parker's 17 leading the way. Redding scored 25 in the next round against Bristol Eastern, but the Hearts let a double-digit lead slip away and were eliminated, 60-59.

Crosby was also knocked out of the L tourney by a team from Bristol in its second game. The Bulldogs had romped past Cheshire, 92-63, behind the versatile Bernie Ireland's 35 points, but then fell to a taller Bristol Central side. Seniors Ireland and Proctor Owens hit double figures for Crosby while Deja Dennis, who transferred to Central from Crosby for that school year, scored 12 points to help eliminate his former Bulldog teammates.

That left Holy Cross to represent the city of Waterbury in CIAC play, and the Crusaders didn't disappoint, advancing the furthest in school history to that point.

The postseason run began with an 84-51 rout of Glastonbury. Junior forwards

Carmen Giampetruzzi and Mike Robinson combnined for 37 points in the next game as the Crusaders cruised past Hall of West Hartford, 90-62, to equal a school-record 21st consecutive win.

Robinson and Bruce Johnson then scored nine points each in the fourth quarter as Holy Cross pulled away from Simsbury, 81-59, to claim the Class LL Region III championship.

The Crusaders started slow in a quarterfinal game against Hillhouse of New Haven, but put together a 13-1 spurt in the third period to outlast the Academics, 72-64, and reach the state semifinals.

A similar scenario played out in the semifinal with Hartford Public, as Holy Cross capitalized on a strong third period to break away from its opponent. The 6-3 Giampetruzzi hit for 33 points and senior center Jeff Weiner added 32 for the Crusaders in the 98-81 victory – a 24th straight win – earning a place in the Class LL title game.

The city high school that claimed its first-ever varsity basketball victory ten years earlier – on January 5, 1971, a 76-64 win over Torrington – had advanced to a CIAC final for this first time in its history, becoming the first Waterbury school to reach a state title game in 14 years (going back to Sacred Heart's Class L title in 1967).

Facing a Wilbur Cross of New Haven team that was playing in its 15th state final in 23 years, the Crusaders kept the game close in the first half. Wilbur Cross controlled things after the intermission with 6-9 Jeff Hoffler recording 24 points and 15 rebounds and junior

Contributed / Holy Cross High School

Holy Cross guard John Burrus drives past Torrington defenders during an NVL game his senior season.

guard Earl Kelley scoring 17 as the Governors prevailed, 80-73, to claim a third straight CIAC title.

Bruce Johnson was named a first-team All-State player (for Class LL), an honor that his two older brothers – Steve and Clay – also received their senior seasons.

He was joined on the All-City team by teammate Burrus, Crosby's Bernie Ireland and the Sacred Heart pair of Darryl Parker and Mark Redding.

Four of the city quintet – Johnson, Burrus, Ireland and Parker – were also part of that year's All-NVL team, along with Jeff Weiner of Holy Cross.

Weiner was presented with the Doc McInerney Award as the top scholar-athlete among city seniors in 1981. Crosby's Ireland, named an All-Stater in Class L, received the Billy Finn Award as the outstanding senior player, while Burrus of Holy Cross was honored with the Lt. Jack Cullinan Award for sportsmanship.

WATR's Allie Vestro: Partner to a pair of Waterbury basketball legends

By the time Holy Cross played Wilbur Cross of New Haven in the 1981 CIAC Class LL final, Waterbury sports fans were accustomed to tuning their radios to WATR – 1320 on the AM dial – to listen to Al Vestro and his crew broadcast the biggest basketball games involving city high school teams each season.

Now 40 years later, the Waterbury-based station is still covering city and NVL hoop contests each winter season. A different set of announcers maintains the tradition of continuous radio coverage that is unmatched in broadcast circles.

Having been treated to decades and decades of scholastic basketball coverage, some fans may wonder when Vestro first started broadcasting high school hoops over the airwaves.

The year was 1947, when Leavenworth High of Waterbury was making a run for the New England schoolboy championship at Boston Garden.

Leavenworth and its star Jimmy Piersall – who would become a major league baseball player – had become the first city school to win a Naugatuck Valley League title that season, but lost to Hillhouse of New Haven in the Class L state final. Despite that result, the Waterbury team was still invited to Boston, as Connecticut was allowed two teams in the New England tournament.

"There was so much interest in the city about this team going to Bos-

Contributed / Sacred Heart High School

Allie Vestro of Sacred Heart watches the ball from under the hoop after completing a drive to the basket against Croft in a 1961 game at the Waterbury Armory. Father Al Vestro can be seen in the WATR radio booth in upper left.

ton to play for the title that my father decided to get a few sponsors and see if he could put a broadcast together," says Al Vestro, Jr., who would join WATR's broadcast team years later. "He had never done a game before, but it came together in a very short period of time. He made all the necessary arrangements and scrambled to get the equipment to do the remote broadcast."

Piersall scored a tournament-record 29 points in the tourney final as Leavenworth defeated Durfee of Fall River, Mass., 51-44, in front of a crowd of 13,909 – reported then as the largest crowd to watch a high school basketball game in New England.

"The game was such a rousing success that the station asked my father if he wanted to do a full schedule of games the following year," recounts Vestro. "At that time there was very little if any television, so people were glued to their radios listening to games, and the broadcasts became such an early success. That it has continued on up until this day is an incredible feat as no other radio station has approached any kind of consecutive record."

Little Allie, as he would become known, was just a youngster when he first joined his father at broadcasts, during another city team's journey to a title.

"I was doing statistics for him on the side in 1953 during Wilby's state championship run, and would have final figures for him before his own crew would have them," notes Vestro, Jr. "Even though I was only 9 years old at the time, I was always very good with numbers, and he decided that he was going to use me to do the stats from that point on."

By then, WATR and its baritone basketball broadcaster had become

fixtures within the city hoop scene, airing doubleheaders a couple of times a week for listeners who couldn't join the thousands of fans crammed into the Waterbury Armory to witness key NVL contests.

And so it began for Allie, who would become an on-air partner to his father two decades later, when the game graduated from the Armory era and moved into a more modern period. WATR's game broadcasts continued their popularity, with Holy Cross' undefeated 1973 season and four different city schools' appearances in state finals in the 1980s providing some highlights for the Vestros' coverage amid the transition.

The WATR legacy continued after Big Al died in 1988, as a number of new voices emerged as partners and replacements for Al Jr., who retired from game broadcasts in 2019. That year, he was made an honorary lifetime member of the New Haven chapter of the International Association of Approved Basketball Officials, the most prestigious award presented by the organization.

Over his many decades behind the microphone, the younger Vestro has described the on-court achievements of some of Waterbury's best-ever players to listeners, including the dominant runs of star-studded Crosby and Sacred Heart teams in the new millennium.

And as each of those seasons neared its end, Vestro would be among the first to announce that year's winner of the Billy Finn Award, given to the top senior player in the city.

As most fans know, the honor is named for the Sacred Heart star of the early 1960s who died in an automobile accident at the age of 18, before being able

The 1960-61 Sacred Heart boys basketball team, coached by Jack Delaney. The starting five included (front row, from left), Tony Moffo, Billy Finn, Bart Cutrali, Al Vestro, Jr. and Jim Morcey.

to showcase his talents at the next level.

What many may not realize is that Finn's backcourt mate during his time at Sacred Heart was one Al Vestro Jr.

Friends since grade-school age, Vestro and Finn "didn't live too far from each other and would meet up to play at Fulton Park many days," remembered Vestro in a 2021 video interview with the Republican-American's Mike Barger. "We would play other sports, but Billy ate, drank and slept basketball. He lived for the sport.

"Billy wasn't the tallest, but he was very quick and had extremely large hands, which allowed him to have so much control of the basketball," continued Vestro in the interview. "He could dribble like Marques Haynes, the famous Globetrotter, and could do magic with the basketball."

Best known for his ball handling skills, Finn "could also shoot with both hands, especially a nice left-handed hook in the lane," adds Vestro.

The long-time broadcaster says he has saved footage of the 1961 game when Finn scored 52 points in a Sacred Heart victory over Naugatuck at the Armory that had fans of both sides raving about his dazzling performance.

"He was uncanny that night, and could not miss," says Vestro. "He was dropping in shots from almost half court that game," a performance that cemented his legacy in city sports lore.

"Billy was just way ahead of his time, in terms of basketball, for his era," says Vestro. "I would have loved to see him play in these times, when players can do so many things."

If the basketball gods ever granted such a request, Allie, here's hoping that you and your father provide the broadcast commentary for that contest!

1981-82: 'Starting Eight' leads Crosby to NVL championship, Class L final

After losing to Wilbur Cross in the 1981 Class LL final, Holy Cross would gain some revenge on the Governors a year later, defeating the New Haven squad 66-65 in a dramatic semifinal to earn a second straight appearance in a CIAC championship game.

The Crusaders were one of two city schools to reach state finals in 1982, as Crosby amassed 25 victories to set a city record for wins in a season while claiming the Naugatuck Valley League title, the Class L Region IV crown and a place in the L championship game.

Despite losing All-State performer Bernie Ireland to graduation, the 1981-82 Bulldogs featured a deep team led by senior Brian Jones. Coach Nick Augelli employed a rotation of players that he dubbed his "starting eight," guiding Crosby to victories in its first four league games before falling in double overtime, 71-70, to Ansonia.

The Bulldogs' running and pressing game kicked back into gear by midseason, as the Old Ivy maintained a slim lead over Ansonia and Holy Cross atop the NVL standings.

A key week in February saw Crosby defeat Sacred Heart, 76-68, to ensure a share of the city title. Jones led the way with 25 points and junior Deja Dennis – who had returned to Crosby after a year at Bristol Central – scored 11 of his 18 points in the decisive third quarter.

Three days later, the Bulldogs (13-1 in the NVL) hosted an 11-2 Holy Cross side at the Palace. Jones again hit for 25 points while 6-1 Jeff Hunter contributed 14 points and 12 rebounds as Crosby held off the Crusaders, 73-65, to clinch a first NVL title for Augelli, who told the *Waterbury Republican* after the game that it was his "greatest win as a coach" to that point in his career.

Ross Annenberg and Jay Clary played key roles in Crosby's final regular-season contests, and the team carried an 11-game winning streak into the league playoffs that involved the top four teams in the standings. Annenberg's free throw with five seconds remaining gave Crosby a 73-72 win over Kennedy in the semifinals before the Bulldogs outlasted Ansonia in the final by a 72-67 margin, as Dennis and Jones combined for 33 points.

With a 21-1 overall record, Crosby was selected as the top seed in the CIAC Class L tournament. Holy Cross, the eighth seed in the LL bracket, was among the four other city schools qualifying for postseason play.

Sacred Heart and Wilby both sprung upsets in opening-round action in the state tournament before falling in their following games. Wilby, seeded 33rd in Class L, ran past sixth-ranked Maloney of Meriden, 89-63, in its opener. The Wildcats then dropped a 73-58 decision to Wilcox Tech; Charles Watson scored a total of 31 points in the Wildcats' two tourney contests.

The Hearts, rated 25th overall in Class M, routed 12th-seeded Farmington, 87-64 in the opener, with five players reaching double figures. Coach Ed Generali's team then took top-seeded Plainville to overtime in the Region III semifinal but were eliminated. Bob Tehan and Thomas Jones combined for 40 points in the 64-62 loss, ending Sacred Heart's season with a 9-13 record.

Kennedy, which received a first-round bye in the Class M tournament, was paired with St. Thomas Aquinas in a Region III semi, a year after the two teams staged a three-overtime thriller in a regional final. Defending M champion Aquinas claimed the rematch, 77-59; the Eagles' John Maia notched 25 points while teammate Waddell Walton hit for 12, surpassing 1,000 points for his scholastic career.

Holy Cross had a pair of seniors – Carmen Giampetruzzi and Mike Robinson – pass the 1,000-point mark during the regular season. The 6-3 forwards led the Crusaders to a 15-5 regular-season record, earning the eighth seed in the Class LL tournament.

In CIAC play, fellow seniors Jim Crocicchia and Steve Schade provided scoring support in victories over Newington and Southington that sent the Crusaders into the Region III final against Hamden. Holy Cross handled the Hamden press, and Robinson and Giampetruzzi scored 19 each in a 59-50 win that secured a second-straight region title.

The senior stars both topped 20 points in the quarterfinals, when the Crusaders canned key free throws down the stretch to hold off Staples, 70-67.

Then came the dramatic semifinal against Wilbur Cross, the three-time defending state champion that had knocked Holy Cross out of the tournament two of the previous three seasons. Trailing by five points in the final minute, the Crusaders reversed what seemed to be another loss to the Governors into an upset victory and a place in the

Contributed / Crosby High School

Members of Crosby's team celebrate the Bulldogs' NVL championship in 1982.

LL final. Giampetruzzi scored 6 of his 30 points in that final minute, including a jumper with six seconds remaining to put Holy Cross up, 66-65. When Wilbur Cross star Earl Kelley (who poured in 35 points) missed a shot at the buzzer, the Crusaders had finally gotten past their New Haven rival.

The LL title game between Holy Cross and Norwalk was tied at 33-all at halftime. But the taller Norwalk team – featuring 6-8 Ray Brown and 6-5 Kevin Stevens, who combined for 56 points on the night – controlled the inside in the second half and held off the Crusaders, 85-76. Robinson hit for 32 points and Giampetruzzi added 24 in their final high-school games.

Giampetruzzi, named an All-State performer in Class LL, was one of two city players to be honored as a first-team

All-State player in 1982. Brian Jones of Crosby also received the nod from the *New Haven Register* after helping to lead the Bulldogs to the Class L championship game.

Crosby's posteason journey began with a 77-51 defeat of Cheshire, with Jones one of four double-figure scorers.

Facing a taller Wilcox Tech team in the Region IV final, the Bulldogs' quickness proved decisive. Deja Dennis collected 16 points, 9 rebounds and 9 assists in the 71-59 victory – which tied a school record for most wins in a season (at 23).

Jeff Hunter's 10 points and block of a potential game-tying jumper were key in Crosby's 54-52 defeat of New London in the state quarterfinals.

Junior guards Jason Williams and Jimmy Kee sank key free throws to secure a 54-44 win over Bristol Central in the next game, giving the Bulldogs their 17th straight victory and a berth in the Class L championship game.

St. Bernard of Uncasville and its 6-6 All-American Harold Pressley proved too tough for Crosby in the LL title game. St. Bernard prevailed, 74-55, in front of an estimated crowd of 3,800 at Central Connecticut's Detrick Gymnasium that included Notre Dame coach Digger Phelps and Villanova's Rollie Massimino.

Dennis had 20 points for Crosby, whose final record of 25-2 represented the most wins in a season in city history. The New Haven Tapoff Club recognized the Bulldogs' stellar season by naming Nick Augelli as its Coach of the Year.

Two Crosby seniors were among the three players honored with the city's annual basketball awards. Ross Annenberg claimed the Doc McInerney Award as top-scholar athlete among seniors in

1982, while Bulldog teammate Brian Jones won the Lt. Jack Cullinan Award for sportsmanship. The Billy Finn Award for outstanding player went to Carmen Giampetruzzi of Holy Cross, who averaged 24 points a game in his senior season.

Giampetruzzi and Mike Robinson of Holy Cross were named first-team All-NVL players, along with Jones of Crosby, Waddell Walton of Kennedy and Ansonia's David Lee.

Jones, Giampetruzzi and Robinson headlined the All-City team for 1982, joined by Fred Carter of Kennedy and Sacred Heart's Thomas Jones.

Contributed / Holy Cross High School

Mike Robinson, seen shooting over a Sacred Heart defender, was selected as both an All-City and All-NVL first-teamer in his senior season.

Looking Back: Carmen Giampetruzzi on the Holy Cross-Wilbur Cross rivalry

As Waterbury schools gained prominence in the post-Armory era while challenging for CIAC tournament glory, each seemed to have a specific, established state power to run up against on numerous occasions during the 1970s and '80s.

Crosby seemed to face off against Warren Harding of Bridgeport regularly in Class L contests during the mid-1970s.

Sacred Heart squared up with the storied St. Thomas Aquinas (of New Britain) program in a number of Class M showdowns in the early '80s.

For Holy Cross, its rivals come tournament time were Hartford Public and the mighty Governors of Wilbur Cross High in New Haven, who dominated the state basketball scene in the 1970s and captured six CIAC LL titles over a ten-year period between 1972 and 1981.

The last of those six titles was an 80-73 triumph over Holy Cross in the 1981 LL championship game. "It was a back-and-forth game and was decided in the last two minutes. Their 6-foot–9 center Jeff Hoffler was the difference," recalls Holy Cross' Carmen Giampetruzzi, who was "fighting the flu that week and played the game with a 103-degree temperature."

Coach Tim McDonald's Crusader team gained revenge a year later by toppling Wilbur Cross at the semifinal stage, with Giampetruzzi scoring three baskets in the final minute of a come-from-behind, one-point victory.

The last two of the 6-foot-3 forward's 30 points came on a game-winning jumper with six seconds remaining, to send Holy Cross into the LL final.

"I have never seen or heard a larger crowd that night at Quinnipiac College," says Giampetruzzi, who was named to the LL All-State team and was the recipient of the Billy Finn Award in 1982.

"Those two tournament games against Wilbur Cross could go down as some of the best back-to-back games in tournament history," believes Giampetruzzi. "The floor was full of future college-bound players and the two coaches (McDonald and Wilbur Cross' Bob Saulsbury) were legends in Connecticut high school hoops.

"I don't know if there were ever four guards of that caliber — Fred Collins and Earl Kelley (of Wilbur Cross) and Bruce Johnson and John Burrus (of Holy Cross) — to match up against each other in a state championship game," continues Giampetruzzi.

The 1980-81 Crusader team was loaded with talent, with senior Jeff Weiner and juniors Giampetruzzi and Mike Robinson rounding out the starting five. "All five of us averaged double-digits. We ran, we pushed the ball, we outscored our opponents at historical marks," adds Giampetruzzi. "I truly believe this team, with five players earning scholarships to college, was one of the better teams to come out of Waterbury."

Giampetruzzi and Robinson, who had played together as teammates since their grade-schools days at St. Mary's School in the city's parochial league, took on bigger roles in their senior season at Holy Cross.

"We were a very different team for the 1981-82 season. We played at a slower pace, but were very smart,"

Contributed / New Hampshire College

Carmen Giampetruzzi went on to star at New Hampshire College after graduating from Holy Cross.

points out Giampetruzzi. "The obvious common denominator was our head coach Tim McDonald. Timmy knew how we could get it done with smart, ball-controlled offense and hard-nosed defense."

The starting five that year was a tough group: "Jim Crocicchia was the quarterback on the football team; Steve Schade was a 6-foot-6 center who was also very intelligent; and Dave Lepore — who everyone now knows from his great food establishment, Roma's — was a great complementary guard who would rarely miss a shot," describes Giampetruzzi.

That 1982 Holy Cross team was "on a roll and finally jelling as a team by the time we faced Wilbur Cross again in the tourney," recalls Giampetruzzi. Earl Kelley was averaging 40 points a game and "Wilbur Cross seemed unstoppable, but with a game plan put together by Tim McDonald and assistants George D'Agostino and Marty DeFazio, we perfected it and came up with a miracle ending."

Wilbur Cross had a five-point lead in the final minute before Giampetruzzi provided the key hoops down the stretch.

The CIAC LL title game between Holy Cross and Norwalk was tied at halftime. But the taller Norwalk side controlled the second half and won, 85-76.

Giampetruzzi, named an All-State performer in Class LL, went on to star at New Hampshire College. A four-year member of the men's basketball team, Giampetruzzi served as co-captain his senior year and help lead the Penmen to a 24-7 record and an appearance in the NCAA Division II Tournament.

Giampetruzzi averaged 21 points a game for his sophomore season, the highest average among New England Division II players that year, and totaled 1,928 career points in his collegiate career. A three-time All-NECC selection, he was voted into his school's Athletic Hall of Fame in 1995.

Moving on to continue his successes in the world of marketing after college, Giampetruzzi still resides in New Hampshire. But the memories of his high school days in Waterbury remain, especially the battles with Catholic school rival Sacred Heart and games against Crosby, which traded NVL titles with Holy Cross over his junior and senior seasons.

"The Sacred Heart vs. Holy Cross games were no less comparable to the Red Sox vs. Yankees," boats Giampetruzzi. "If you look at old pictures, our crowds were so big that we had to re-locate the games to a bigger gym at Crosby High School. And we had some memorable games with Crosby."

Crosby would also reach a CIAC final in 1982. The next season, Sacred Heart and Wilby would each advance to CIAC championship games before falling at the final hurdle.

The Hearts would end the string of title-game losses by city teams when it routed Weston to win the 1984 Class M crown.

But, win or lose – as Giampetruzzi notes – the early 1980s produced some of the more memorable moments and best basketball teams in the city's history.

1982-83: Wilby, Sacred Heart represent city in CIAC title games

One year after three NVL basketball teams captured region championships in the CIAC tournament, another trio produced long runs in the 1983 state tourney as city and league teams continued their rise in prominence within Connecticut hoop circles.

Ansonia, with a number of its top players returning from a squad that reached the Class M semifinals, became the first non-city team to win the NVL title in 14 years by claiming the 1982-83 league crown.

Coach Tom McQueeney's Chargers featured an impressive frontline, led by 6-4 Marcus Garris and 6-2 Gordie Hotchkiss, and stormed through a 15-1 league campaign – with the lone loss a 62-61 decision at home to defending NVL champ Crosby.

Holding a slim one-game lead in the standings over Wilby late in the season, Ansonia claimed a pair of two-point victories over Sacred Heart and Wilby to clinch the league title.

Hotchkiss and John Lawlor combined for 29 points while Garris hit the winning basket with nine seconds remaining in the 63-61 decision over the Hearts.

The showdown with Wilby went to overtime before the Chargers prevailed. Hotchkiss scored with ten seconds remaining to force the extra session and then canned six free throws as Ansonia held on for a 59-57 home win.

With the NVL title in hand and an 18-2 overall record, Ansonia earned the top seed in the CIAC Class M tournament. The Chargers defeated Whitney

Tech and Middletown to win the Region IV title. Hotchkiss then scored 22 points in a 73-50 win over New Milford before the Chargers were eliminated by St. Thomas Aquinas in the M semifinals – the third straight year that Ansonia would be knocked out of the state tournament by the Saints.

The Aquinas victory prevented an all-NVL final, as Sacred Heart had maneuvered its way through the M bracket to reach the title game at Central Connecticut State University. Coach Ed Generali's Hearts had finished tied for third in the league standings and were seeded 10th overall in the M division.

Sacred Hearts faced a familiar foe in the first round, topping city rival Kennedy, 73-51, with juniors Anthony Perry and Calvin Glenn combining for 43 points. Junior center Henry Brown, with 29 points and 14 rebounds, and senior Pete Tehan, with 17 points, paced the Hearts to victory in the next game, an 88-77 decision over Farmington.

In the Region III final, Sacred Heart was beaten by St. Thomas Aquinas, 65-57, but still advanced to the M quarterfinals thanks to the CIAC tourney format allowing both region finalists to move on.

With that second life, the Hearts built up an early lead on New London and held on for a 59-50 win in the quarterfinals. Perry hit for 25 points in that game and followed with a 21-point effort in the semifinal, when Sacred Heart needed overtime to eliminate Kolbe-Cathedral of Bridgeport, 67-62.

In its first state final since 1967, Sacred Heart met St. Thomas Aquinas in a re-

Contributed / Wilby High School

Marty Hayre, Billy Finn Award winner for the 1982-83 season, scores on a driving layup for Wilby.

match of the Region III final. The New Britain team's inside-outside duo of Josh Farrell and Carl Miazga kept the Hearts from claiming the third state title in school history, as Aquinas pulled away for a 73-57 win and a third consecutive Class M championship.

Wilby was also eliminated at the final hurdle after producing a impressive 1982-83 season. Coach Bob Freeman's Wildcats featured the tallest frontline in the NVL – with 6-7 James Saunders, 6-4 Marty Hayre and 6-3 Prathon Battle – and had battled Ansonia throughout the season for top spot in the standings before losing two games late in February.

Seeded 9th overall in Class L, Wilby ousted Kaynor Tech in its tourney opener as Hayre and junior guard Frank Locke each topped 20 points on the night.

Saunders collected 16 points and 22 rebounds and senior Wayne Williams added 18 as the Wildcats then dispatched Maloney, 93-74.

The Region IV final was a low-scoring affair, with Hayre netting 23 of his team's 38 points in a victory over Platt of Meriden for the region crown.

In the M quarterfinals, Wilby was trailing by 12 points after three periods before staging a dramatic comeback against Masuk of Monroe. Hayre scored eight fourth-quarter points in the 65-63 victory, with Mike Yeldell's two free throws with eight seconds remaining providing the winning margin.

The Wildcats' semifinal proved just as suspenseful; freshman Ted McIntosh hit a layup and converted two free throws in the final 35 seconds as Wilby outlasted Hartford Bulkeley, 56-55. The fifth straight victory resulted in the school's third appearance in a state final.

Victorious in those two prior appearances, Wilby could not get past an undefeated Warren Harding team, featuring 6-9 All-American Charles Smith, in the Class L final. Smith and game MVP Marvin Gray led the undefeated Presidents to a 58-51 win, ending Wilby's season at 19-6.

Hayre, who scored 14 points in the state final and earned All-State status in Class L, claimed the Billy Finn Award as outstanding player among city seniors for the 1982-83 season. Joe Pettit of Crosby was honored as top scholar-athlete with the Doc McInerney Award, and Sacred Heart's Rich Greene won the Lt. Jack Cullinan Award for sportsmanship.

The All-City team for 1982-83 included Wilby's Hayre along with Jay Clary of Crosby, Sacred Heart's Anthony Perry, Vern Riddick of Kennedy and Holy Cross sophomore Kelly Monroe, who had the highest scoring average in league games.

Hayre and Monroe were the lone representatives from city teams on the All-NVL first team for 1982-83. Marcus Garris and Gordie Hotchkiss of league champion Ansonia made the team, along with 6-1 senior Allan Bredice of Torrington.

Looking back: Wilby's 1923 squad was first city team to win a CIAC title

Wilby High's run to the 1983 Class L title game marked the third time in school history that the Wildcats appeared in a state championship game.

The three occasions happened to each be spaced out exactly 30 years apart – in 1923, 1953 and 1983 – with Wilby taking home the trophy on the first two appearances.

The initial title win came prior to the founding of the Naugatuck Valley League – which happens to be the oldest scholastic athletic conference in Connecticut – and when the rules of the game called for a jump ball at the center circle after every basket was scored.

Wilby wasn't as highly regarded in 1923 as Crosby's team, which had completed its second consecutive regular season without a loss. But the highly-regarded Bulldogs, led by captain Alden White, had aspirations beyond state borders. They were off in Philadelphia, attempting to defend their regional title at the University of Pennsylvania tournament – two years after finishing third at the National Interscholastic Championship in Chicago.

The Green & White of Wilby weren't even included in the initial group of 16 teams chosen for the Yale Interscholastic Tournament, which served as the competition to determine Connecticut's champion that year.

Wilby accepted an invitation from state organizers after a number of schools declined to participate. The team took full advantage of the opportunity, advancing all the way to the final, where it defeated Naugatuck, 21-20.

The championship game went down to the final seconds, when Wilby's Michael "Mickey" Hayes sank a shot from distance to beat the buzzer and complete a last-minute rally. Wilby captain Tim Murphy had converted a free throw moments earlier to cut the deficit to a point, before Hayes gained possession from the ensuing jump ball to launch his heroic heave and delight Wildcat fans in attendance at the Yale gymnasium.

"It was one of the original 'Hail Mary' shots," Hayes said, when asked to remember the game for a *Republican-American* article in March of 1989. "I recall getting the ball near the center circle, turning around and taking a two-handed set shot right before the whistle," added Hayes, who became a truant officer for Waterbury schools before eventually moving to Rhode Island.

Hayes and his 1923 Wilby teammates have all died, but the team's legacy remains as not only Waterbury's first CIAC basketball champions, but also as the first CIAC title winners decided on the court. The state's governing body was founded in 1921 and had declared Naugatuck High as its state basketball champion for that 1921-22 school year, based on its season record rather than an elimination tournament.

Wilby opened the 1923 tourney with an impressive win over Rockville in the first round. Captain Murphy and fellow forward Hal Hadley combined for 12 field goals in Wilby's 42-18 victory. The win came one day after city rival Crosby was knocked out of the Penn tournament by Scott High of Toledo, leaving the Green and White as Waterbury's sole remaining team to claim a tournament prize of any kind in 1923.

Hadley led the way for Wilby in the

Wilby's 1923 state champions are pictured with the trophy after winning the first state tournament conducted by the CIAC that year. Standing, from left, are captain Tim Murphy and coach Frank 'Chief' Borden. Sitting, front row from left: Harold 'Hal' Hadley, Tom 'Red' Navin, James O'Neill and Maurice 'Zeke' Connors. Back row, from left, Berkelee Sperring, Matt Holloway (manager) and Michael Hayes. Missing from photo: Ebbie Conlan.

second round, netting 10 points in an 18-7 triumph over Meriden High that earned coach Frank Borden's team a place in the semifinals.

The semifinals and final of the tournament at Yale – which were both played on the same day – proved to be much tougher contests for Wilby. Guard James O' Neill played a key role in the Saturday morning semifinal against Commercial High of New Haven, scoring the winning hoop in the closing seconds of a 20-18 decision.

The afternoon final was another close affair. Wilby's defensive ace Thomas "Red" Navin held Naugatuck captain Bill Harvey to one field goal for the game, but the Greyhounds used a fourth-quarter surge to take a two-point lead into the final minute.

Even after Murphy's free throw cut the deficit to 20-19 with seconds remaining, Naugatuck still looked more likely to raise the trophy. Instead, it was Wilby's versatile substitute Hayes who would be raised upon his teammates' shoulders after sinking the incredible game- and title-winning shot.

"Was I a hero?" pondered Hayes in his 1989 comments. "I guess so. Now, when they have the tournament, I remember that game. It is a nice memory."

Another reserve player on Wilby's state title-winning team was Edward "Ebbie" Conlan, who would go on to coach the city's next CIAC champion. He guided Sacred Heart to the 1949 Class B crown, defeating Darien in the final, to become the only person to play on and coach state title-winning teams from Waterbury.

Recalling his playing days in that same *Republican-American* article from 1989, Conlan noted the differences in the sport over time – including the size of the ball, which was originally "much larger; it had laces on it and was harder to shoot. ... Basketball was a whole lot different then," he said.

There may have been some differences but, as evidenced by Wilby's 1923 state championship run, those early years were no different to the modern game in producing the types of thrilling moments and experiences that would go on to serve as lifelong memories for participants and fans alike.

1983-84: Sacred Heart wins city's first state crown in 17 years

The race for the 1983-84 Naugatuck Valley League basketball crown came down to a battle between three city teams, with Sacred Heart, Holy Cross and Kennedy all tied at the top in mid-February.

The Hearts, who had reached the Class M final a year earlier and featured a number of returning starters, were considered favorites to claim the title. But the other two teams in contention were coming off losing seasons in 1982-83 and produced impressive campaigns, resulting in a dramatic final month of basketball.

After a 6-14 showing in 1982-83, Holy Cross returned the bulk of its squad that included 6-4 junior Kelly Monroe, who had led the league in scoring as a sophomore. Kennedy, which endured a 10-11 record the previous year, featured 6-4 seniors Vern Riddick and Billy Evans to lead the Eagles' challenge against city rivals.

The Hearts cruised through the first half of the the league season with a 7-1 record that included a comeback win over defending NVL champion Ansonia after trailing by double digits. Calvin Glenn hit for 30 points in that game and followed it with 31 in an 88-65 rout of Crosby four nights later.

A Sacred Heart loss to Naugatuck allowed Holy Cross to take over the top spot in the league standings in the first week of February, when the Crusaders claimed two roads wins – edging Ansonia, 68-66, on two free throws by guard Frank Lombardo with four seconds remaining, and topping Torrington, 67-49, behind Monroe's 27 points.

Holy Cross' six-game win streak came to an end in its next league outing, as Sacred Heart produced one of its best efforts of the season to run past the Crusaders, 68-47, in a game played at the Crosby Palace. Anthony Perry and Glenn each netted 19 points to lead Coach Ed Generali's Hearts, avenging an early-season loss to the Crusaders.

Four nights later, Kennedy defeated Naugatuck, 59-53, to improve to 11-2 in the NVL – the identical record of both Sacred Heart and Holy Cross – to secure a temporary three-way tie at the top of the NVL standings. Vern Riddick scored 21 points and point guard Neal Ware added 15 for the Eagles, who survived the back-and-forth affair with a strong fourth quarter.

Sacred Heart needed a buzzer-beating jump shot by Perry to nip Wilby in its next game, the second time the senior guard had delivered a game-winning bucket as time expired that season.

Wilby then played a role in determining a regular-season champion by upsetting Holy Cross, 61-53, in its next outing.

The Hearts capitalized by routing Torrington, 90-59, and clinched the city and NVL championships by holding off Kennedy, 56-55. Coach Jack Taglia's Eagles used a deliberate pace to claim an early lead in that game, but Glenn and Perry combined for 32 points in the comeback victory.

With a 16-4 overall record, Sacred Heart was ranked fifth in the CIAC Class M tournament. Kennedy, also finishing with a 16-4 record, was seeded sixth in the L bracket, while Holy Cross

(17-3) earned the third overall spot in the LL tourney.

Holy Cross topped the century mark in running past West Haven, 103-85, in its LL West Region II opener. Monroe collected 33 points and 13 rebounds while Lombardo, Kenny Green and reserve James Monroe also reached double figures.

The Crusaders started slow in their next outing, and a second-half comeback fell short against 15th-seeded Danbury. Monroe hit for 16 points and Steve Northrop scored 10 for Holy Cross in the 65-50 loss.

Kennedy's postseason run also lasted just two games. The Eagles cruised past Abbott Tech – with Riddick and Billy Evans each scoring 18 points – in the region opener, before falling to Bassick of Bridgeport, 58-51, and ending the

Seniors on Sacred Heart's 1983-84 team that won the Class M title included, back row from left: Ossie Mejil, Henry Brown, Dave Franks and Calvin Glenn; and kneeling: Craig Wood and Anthony Perry.

Contributed / Crosby High School

Kenny Green of Holy Cross rises to block a shot by Crosby's Don Trottie in a game at Crosby during the 1983-84 season.

1983-84 campaign with a 17-5 record.

A Bridgeport team was the opening opponent for Sacred Heart's run in the Class M tournament. The Hearts received a scare from an 8-12 Kolbe-Cathedral squad before prevailing, 62-57. Big men Henry Brown, who scored 18 points, and Dave Franks hit late free throws to secure the win.

Sacred Heart fell behind its next two opponents before rallying for victories. Glenn led the way with 27 points in an 84-67 triumph over Immaculate in the Class M West Region II second round. In the next round, the 6-5 Brown netted 28 points and the Hearts outscored Weston 23-6 in the third period to win goinng away, 78-57, and claim the region trophy, a first for the school.

In the quarterfinal, seniors Perry, Glenn and Brown all topped 20 points as Sacred Heart held off St. Joseph of Trumbull to earn a rematch against nemesis St. Thomas Aquinas of New Britain, which defeated the Hearts in a regular-season contest and in the M

final one season earlier.

Sacred Heart's strong inside game proved the difference in the semifinal. Glenn, Brown and Franks combined for 50 points in a 78-70 triumph, avenging those two previous losses and ending Aquinas' attempt at a fourth consecutive state title.

The CIAC Class M final was a rematch of the West Region II final, but it was not much of a contest as Sacred Heat ran Weston out of the Central Connecticut State University gym.

The Hearts built an early 24-6 lead and contained Weston's pair of 6-5 sophomores, Don Polite and Tony Jackson, to claim the school's and the city's first state title since 1967 – when Coach Ed Generali was himself a player in Sacred Heart's program and its varsity team had defeated Fairfield Prep for the Class L crown.

Glenn notched 24 points and 9 rebounds in the 72-48 victory, while tournament MVP Perry scored 23 points, including the 1,000th points of his high school career.

Both Hearts' players were named to the All-City and All-NVL first teams for the 1983-84 season. Perry and Glenn were joined on the All-City team by repeat selections Kelly Monroe of Holy Cross and Vern Riddick of Kennedy, along with Kaynor Tech's Darryl Lovett – who surpassed 1,000 points for his career in a midseason win over Platt of Meriden.

The All-NVL first team included city stars Perry, Glenn, Monroe and Riddick, along with sharpshooter Keith Rado of Naugatuck, who averaged 22 points a game for the Greyhounds.

Perry and Riddick also received two of the three annual awards presented to city seniors. The Sacred Heart guard was honored with the Billy Finn Award as the most outstanding player in Waterbury. Kennedy's Riddick was presented with the Lt. Jack Cullinan Award for sportsmanship, and Art Burrus of Crosby was recipient of the Doc McInerney Award as top scholar-athlete among city seniors.

Contributed / Wilby High School

Frank Locke and Wilby upset Kelly Monroe and Holy Cross late in the season, a result that helped give the 1984 NVL to Sacred Heart.

Generali: Hearts' 1984 title 'broke the ice,' proved Waterbury belonged on big stage

Sacred Heart's victory over Weston to claim the 1984 Class M crown represented the third state title in school history, after having captured CIAC championships in 1949 and 1967.

Ed Generali, head coach of the 1984 champs, was a member of the Hearts' junior varsity team in 1967, when coach John Gilmore guided a talented squad featuring Joe Summa and Don Sasso to a Class L title.

"I was strictly a JV player. However, I got to practice every day with the varsity and had the pleasure of guarding big Don Sasso – all 6 foot, 8 inches of him – on a daily basis. There were many lessons to be learned for sure," quips Generali. "As it turns out, Sasso and Ned Cunningham, members of the 1967 team, became two of my closest friends and they along with John Gilmore were at the game in 1984 cheering us on and sharing in the celebration later."

Generali considers Gilmore one of the most influential people in his life. "I was a Boys' Club kid and John began his coaching career there, with one of the state age-group teams. When I made the Hearts as a sophomore John had taken over as varsity coach and despite his stature we were all in awe, and sometimes fear, of him," says Generali, who would go on to serve as an assistant to Gilmore prior to taking over as head coach for the 1979-80 season.

"John's intensity and knowledge

Ed Generali

of the game was immense," recalls Generali. "We would go eat after games, and he would pull coins out of his pocket and start to diagram plays for the next game. He was the perfect mentor for me."

When Gilmore retired, "he left me with my returning JV team, which was very talented but young," remembers Generali. "He knew it would provide a good transition since I had already been coaching that group. We didn't have to change much from what John had done with the previous group and it helped lead to us winning the league that initial year."

Three years later, Generali's team reached the Class M final, falling to perennial state power St. Thomas Aquinas. "I really believe that the 1983 team that reached the Class M title game set the table for the1984 championship," says Generali. "I felt bad that a few of our seniors in 1983, mainly Pete Tehan and Rich Greene, were such great team players but didn't get a piece of the net. I was happy to see that they were both present the following year when we did win."

Sacred Heart's 1983-84 team had the key components of a championship side, according to its coach. "We had all the positions covered: a great point guard in Anthony Perry, a shooter in Craig Wood, a super power forward in Calvin Glenn, two big men in Henry Brown and David Frank, and then a transfer in Ozzie Mejil

Sacred Heart players and coaches celebrate the 1984 CIAC Class M title after defeating Weston in the championship game.

who just complemented them all," notes Generali – who would go on to coach Holy Cross to two state titles (in 1995 and 2000) and have the Crusaders' home court dedicated in his name in 2017.

"Believe it or not, when that 1983-84 group were sophomores, we were struggling. And after one tough loss, they promised me a state championship before they graduated," recalls Generali. "And while it was a dream team, their senior year also started poorly … we lost four games early, but they re-dedicated themselves and we didn't lose again," says Generali

Victories the rest of the way in that memorable 1983-84 season included a defeat of nemesis St. Thomas Aquinas, which was aiming for a fourth consecutive state title.

The revenge factor may have played a part, with Aquinas having beaten Sacred Heart twice in the 1983 tournament. But the Hearts had won a matchup between the two in the Pearl Street Holiday Fes-

tival, which gave Generali's squad some confidence in facing a vaunted opponent.

"I give much credit to the Pearl St. Summer League and its Holiday Festival, which encouraged us to bring power-house teams from throughout the state to compete with our kids," notes Generali. "I even recall the trips that Pearl Street director Hubie Williamson used to arrange, to bring Waterbury players to compete in other parts of the country."

Kennedy coach Jack Taglia joined Generali on one memorable trip, to the University of North Carolina, when the two guided an all-star team and competed against all-stars from that area.

Such experiences during that period proved beneficial for players and teams from Waterbury, as evidenced by four different city schools reaching CIAC title games in the early 1980s, along with Sacred Heart's championship.

"I feel our 1984 team 'broke the ice' and proved Waterbury basketball belonged on the big stage."

1984-85: Crosby takes top spot in season marked by tragedy

The 1984-85 high school basketball season in Waterbury was marked by tragedy during the preseason, when Wilby player Robert Donaldson drowned in the school's pool after a Saturday practice in early December.

Devastated by the loss of a teammate, the Wildcats team also learned soon after that the basketball program would be suspended for a time by city schools superintendent Paul Duffy. Coach Bob Freeman and assistant David Kalach were relieved of their duties for failing to supervise players the day of the

Contributed / Holy Cross High School

Kelly Monroe of Holy Cross looks to score on a fast break against Crosby.

drowning, and Wilby was not allowed to practice or play until mid-January — forfeiting half of its games scheduled for the season.

Reggie O'Brien, a teacher at Wilby who was also coach at Post College in Waterbury, was selected from among a number of applicants to take over as the school's head coach. The young Wildcats, who would feature a sophomore and freshman among the starters in most games, were finally able to open their season on Jan. 25 after just six practice sessions with their new coach.

"We have been through an awful lot the last six weeks, and we are ready to go now," senior co-captain DeWitt McCormick told the *Waterbury Republican* prior to the opener, a road game at Torrington. "We're just going to play together as a team with unity for the new coach and for Rob. It will be a big relief for us to go out on the court and clear our minds."

Wilby was defeated in that initial contest, but rebounded five days later to hold off Sacred Heart, 86-84, at home to claim victory for the first time. Freshman Phil Lott scored 30 points in the win, one of three victories in the Wildcats' shortened season.

By that point in the league campaign, city foes Crosby and Holy Cross had emerged as the main contenders for the Naugatuck Valley League title.

The teams took identical 5-0 league records into a mid-January battle at The Pit, with the Bulldogs emerging as a 58-52 victor over the hosts — who were ranked fifth in the state at the time.

Members of the 1984-85 All-NVL first team included: front row, from left, Crosby's Willie Davis and Kelly Monroe of Holy Cross; and back row, Tom Patulak of Ansonia, Torrington's Murray Williams and Kenny Green of Holy Cross.

Crosby guard Tracy Jones hit some key hoops down the stretch in the road win, which coach Nick Augelli credited to solid team defense and the strong inside presence of 6-6 center Willie Davis – who emerged as one of the NVL's top players in his junior season.

Crosby had posted a 4-16 record the previous season but returned four starters and a host of players with varsity experience to complement Davis. Senior Darryl Harris was the primary ballhandler while classmates Don Trottie and Mike Pekock added depth in the frontcourt as the Bulldogs cruised through the first half of its schedule (dropping just two non-league contests, both to a tough Hamden team).

Led by All-State performer Kelly Monroe and its own 6-foot-7 big man, Kenny Green, Holy Cross would keep pace with Crosby throughout much of the league season. Key Crusader wins included a 43-42 victory at Kennedy, with senior guard Frank Lombardo hitting a buzzer-beating jumper to send the game into overtime and converting a pair of foul shots in the extra session that provided the winning points.

Crosby had a buzzer-beating hero of its own, when Darryl Harris scored from close range to avoid overtime and hand Naugatuck a 61-59 defeat. The result helped ensure that the Crosby-Holy Cross rematch would essentially decide the NVL title.

That decider in late February was played in front of a crowd of over 2,000 at the Crosby Palace, with the host Bulldogs opening a first-half lead that grew into double figures by the third period.

With Crusader Ken Green limited

1984-85 NVL champion Crosby Bulldogs

by foul trouble, Willie Davis and Don Trottie combined for 40 points on the night as Crosby held off a late Holy Cross rally to prevail, 56-54, and clinch a share of the league crown.

The 6-foot-4 Monroe scored 26 in the loss, and then hit for 20 points in an 89-55 home win over Wilby to break Spencer Harrison's record of 1,290 career points and become the all-time scoring leader at Holy Cross.

Crosby went on to lose an overtime game at Ansonia – a first defeat in league play – before trouncing Wilby, 112-69, in its final regular-season contest to give coach Nick Augelli his second NVL championship in six years as head coach.

With a 16-4 record, Crosby earned the fifth overall seed in the Class L tournament and the second spot in the West Region II. Kaynor Tech of Waterbury, which captured the Inter-County Athletic Conference title and was led by Rufus Freeman and Doug Riddick, was slotted right behind Crosby in the L West Region, but fell to Naugatuck in its CIAC opener.

Crosby received an opening-round bye and then fought off Masuk, 71-53, with Davis collecting 18 points and 16 rebounds and Harris and Alan Piccolo reaching double figures.

Davis then produced one of his better outings as the Bulldogs trounced Bunnell of Stratford to claim the L West Region II trophy. The 6-7 center finished with 33 points, 24 rebounds and five blocked shots as Crosby pulled away for a 76-52 victory.

The Bulldogs' tournament run came to an end in the L quarterfinal, a physical battle between two 18-4 teams that required overtime to be decided. Crosby had a 12-point lead on 4th-seeded Plainville but needed a Davis tip-in to force the extra session.

A three-point play by Darryl Harris gave Crosby a 63-62 lead with 50 seconds left in overtime, but Plainville's Mark Czerepusko converted a second-chance effort in the closing seconds to give his team a one-point victory.

"I can't be happy with the loss but we had a great season and the players can be proud," coach Nick Augelli told the *Waterbury Republican*'s Roger Cleveland after the game. "We turned our record around after going 4-16 last season. We won the city, we won the league, and we won the region. It was an unbelievable season; the players worked really hard."

Like Crosby, Holy Cross took a 16-4 regular-season record into the CIAC tournament. The Crusaders, seeded sixth in Class LL, received an opening-round bye in the West I Region bracket.

Monroe, Green and Lombardo all topped 20 points in Holy Cross' first CIAC outing, an impressive 82-58 rout of Fairfield Prep. The 6-7 Green then notched 27 points and 17 rebounds in a 70-64 triumph over Stamford to earn a place in the region final.

Facing a 13-9 Bridgeport Central team that had upset the region's top-seed Brien McMahon, the Crusaders cruised to victory behind a stellar performance from Kelly Monroe. The senior forward contributed 30 points and 13 points and Holy Cross claimed the LL West Region I crown via the 78-59 win.

That 18th victory would be the last of the season for Holy Cross, who battled Newington into double overtime before dropping a 66-64 decision in the LL quarterfinals. Monroe scored 21 points in his final high-school game, to finish second (behind Steve Johnson of Crosby) on the city's all-time career scoring list with 1,477 points.

The Boston College-bound Monroe, again the league's top scorer (with a

Contributed / Crosby High School

Crosby guard Daryl Harris, recipient of the Lt. Jack Cullinan Award for the 1984-85 season, pulls up against Holy Cross' Frank Lombardo, the Doc McInerny Award winner that season.

23 ppg average), was named the 1985 recipient of the Billy Finn Award, while Holy Cross teammate Frank Lombardo earned the Doc McInerney Award as top scholar among city seniors. Crosby guard Daryl Harris received the city's sportsmanship award, named in honor of Lt. Jack Cullinan.

The Crosby pair of Willie Davis and Don Trottie joined Monroe as first team All-City players for the 1984-85 season. Chris Love of Kennedy and Kaynor Tech big man Rufus Freeman rounded out the quintet.

The All-City second team consisted of Ken Green and Frank Lombardo of Holy Cross, Crosby guard Daryl Harris, Chis O'Toole of Sacred Heart and Kennedy's Vin Riddick.

Monroe and Davis also headlined the All-NVL team. Holy Cross' Kenny Green was also selected to the first team, along with Ansonia's Tom Patulak and Torrington sophomore Murray Williams.

Piccolo remembers title season

"To this day, every time I walk into the Crosby gym, I always find myself looking at the 1984-1985 NVL championship banner and remembering a great group of teammates," says Alan Piccolo, the current Wilby High head coach, who was a junior guard on that Bulldog team.

"I still have many fond memories of playing with that group," recalls Piccolo. "And the support of the student body for games every Tuesday and Friday night was electrifying."

In front of perhaps the biggest crowd at the Crosby Palace that year, the Bulldogs defeated rival Holy Cross for a late February victory that clinched a share of that season's league crown, with Willie Davis and 'Dondi' Trottie combining for 40 points on the night.

The Bulldogs claimed the league title outright with a win over Wilby in the regular-season finale. Nick Augelli's team then went on to claim a Class L West Region II trophy in the state tournament before being eliminated in the quarterfinal round.

To get an idea about the makeup of that championship team, according to Piccolo, "you really need to look at the previous year's team. He notes that in 1983-84, Crosby's squad was an extremely young team with only one senior, Art Burrus. A quartet of juniors – Daryl Harris, Cary Lucian, Mike Pekock and Trottie – were among the regulars for coach Nick Augelli, along with sophomores Davis and Piccolo, and freshman Tracey Jones.

"We played like a young team and finished 4-16, but we all gained valuable experience," remembers Piccolo. "For me, it was us going 4-16 that really drove me to get better. I think it had that effect on all of us."

With each player improving his game and "our team chemistry growing – as many of us had been playing together for two or three seasons – we felt we would be competitive in 1984-85," says Piccolo. "This was also the year that Willie Davis really came out of his shell and turned into one of the best players in the league, if not the state."

Alan Piccolo

The 6-7 Davis became a force on the inside for Crosby. And, "combined with the point guard play of Daryl Harris and the shooting of 'Dondi,' we were a good team," adds Piccolo. "We were a hard team to defend because we got up and down the floor and had many options."

An early-season win at 5-0 Holy Cross – featuring Kelly Monroe and Kenny Green and ranked among the state's top ten teams at the time – gave the Crosby team some confidence and a place atop the league standings, which it maintained through the clinching games noted above.

Aiming for a repeat in Piccolo's senior season, Crosby was among the NVL favorites going into the 1985-86 campaign. "But Wilby had other ideas and finished 18-2 and won the city and league titles," says Piccolo. "It was disappointing, but something that we had done to ourselves by losing three games in a row at one point of the season."

That year, Crosby and Wilby were both classified as Class L schools, and "we were happy to see that we were heading into the state tournament with a chance to face Wilby again," says Piccolo. "Coach Augelli warned us not to look past Foran in the first round, but I can honestly tell you that all of us were looking ahead!"

Piccolo remembers Augelli's words to the team after beating Foran. "He put it to us this way: 'Since we split our two games during the season, whichever team wins this next one would be the better team.'

"That motivated me. But we knew that game wasn't going to be easy," Piccolo says of the CIAC second-round encounter with Wilby. "Phil Lott was a load to try and defend. He had size, strength, and speed. Kevin Eason was also strong on the boards."

Davis sparked Crosby to an early lead before Wilby recovered behind Lott and Eason, who combined for 49 points on the night. With the game tied with a minute-and-a-half remaining, Tracey Jones converted a three-point play, and Piccolo then scored the next six points to secure an 89-83 victory for the Bulldogs.

"Tracey Jones played an unbelievable game. He was the most underrated man on our team," notes Piccolo. "At the end of the game, it was my turn to contribute to the team win by hitting a few shots and some free throws. It was nice to oust them from the tournament and move on."

Two rounds later, Piccolo scored a career-high 30 points as Crosby defeated top-seeded Middletown to reach the Class L semifinals. The Bulldogs were eliminated at that stage by Warren Harding of Bridgeport, which went on to win its fourth consecutive Class L title.

Piccolo credits Augelli and his assistant coaches – Ed Snow, Dennis Sullivan and Bill Mahoney – for impacting his development throughout his scholastic career.

"Ed Snow is one of the best shooters I ever knew, and the one that taught me how to shoot. And Dennis Sullivan was the first coach to teach me about team unity and team pride," adds Piccolo. "I owe each of them for what they have taught me."

Piccolo says that Augelli has also played a huge role in his coaching career. "He was the one that offered me my first coaching position, – freshman basketball coach at Crosby." Piccolo remained in that position for 10 years until being named varsity coach at Wilby in 2007.

Augelli's "defensive approach to the game is something that I try to continue to this day," notes Piccolo. "And I think the greatest impact that he left on me was how he showed that he cared for his players. As a player, you could always count on him."

Contributed / Crosby High School

Alan Piccolo releases a jumper over a Holy Cross defender. Piccolo was named to the *Republican-American's* All-City team for the 1985-86 season.

Supporting their teams:
Cheerleaders from the 1980s

Contributed / Holy Cross High School

Contributed / Kennedy High School

Contributed / Crosby High School

Contributed / Kaynor Tech High School

Contributed / Wilby High School

Contributed / Sacred Heart High School

Contributed / Holy Cross High School

Contributed / Crosby High School

Contributed / Sacred Heart High School

Contributed / Kaynor Tech High School

Contributed / Wilby High School

1985-86: Lott and Eason lead Wilby to school's first NVL title in 12 years

A iming to become the first team to repeat as Naugatuck Valley League champion in nearly a decade, Crosby opened the 1985-86 season as favorite for the league title, as perennial rival Holy Cross had lost its top three players from the previous season – including the school's all-time scoring leader Kelly Monroe – to graduation.

But considering the competitive nature of the league, Crosby coach Nick Augelli realized how tough such an accomplishment would be.

"It is a major task to repeat as the NVL basketball champ," he noted in comments included among city coaches' preseason views in the *Waterbury Republican*'s season preview article published in December 1985. "Every game the pressure wears on you, because everyone wants to knock off the favorite. This will be a mind-testing season, because every team will play at its best against us."

Big man Willie Davis was back for his senior season at Crosby, with senior guard Alan Piccolo providing scoring from the outside and Tracy Jones and Nate Ervin adding support for Augelli's troops.

The Bulldogs' defense of the league crown started impressively with wins in 10 of their first 11 NVL games.

But Crosby then suffered two straight one-point losses — away to Torrington and to Sacred Heart at The Palace — that turned the tide in the league race and gave Wilby a chance to claim the NVL trophy.

High-scoring swingman Phil Lott took on a bigger role in his sophomore season at Wilby, as Coach Reggie O' Brien's Wildcats relied on their speed and athleticism to run past opponents. Five-foot-three senior Ted McIntosh and junior forward Kevin Eason also played major roles for a WIlby team looking to claim the school's first league title in 12 years.

By late February, Wilby had surged past Crosby at the top of the NVL standings. With Lott averaging close to 23 points a game in league contests, the Wildcats stood at 11-2 in the league and held a one-game lead over the Bulldogs.

Eason and Lott combined for 41 points as Wilby defeated Naugatuck, 73-60, in its next outing, on the same night an underdog Holy Cross team upset Crosby to widen Wilby's margin at the top of the league.

Seniors Kevin McGetrick and Tim Drakeley each topped 20 points to lead Tim McDonald's Crusaders to their fourth straight victory, on a night when Holy Cross also broke the Crosby junior varsity team's 31-game win streak.

Wilby then cinched the NVL title in dramatic fashion in its next contest. Jack Taglia's Kennedy team controlled the tempo in a low-scoring affair that was tied at 41 with one minute remaining. Host Wilby then held possession in the closing moments, before Lott lofted a shot from 18 feet out that swished through the net as the final buzzer sounded.

"It is a real credit to the kids, to wrap up the title here and take away some of the importance of the final game against Crosby," O'Brien would tell the *Republican-American* reporter Roger Cleaveland after the 43-41 victory. "I knew that we had a good bunch of kids, but I was hoping for a 12-8 or 13-7 record at best. I never dreamed that we would win the NVL title."

Before playing the season-ender against Crosby, Wilby faced the city's technical school, Kaynor Tech – which featured Waterbury's top scorer on the season in 6-4 Rufus Freeman.

Averaging more than 30 points and 20 rebounds a contest, Freeman had led the Panthers to the top of the Inter-County Athletic Conference standings for a

Contributed / Wilby High School

Phil Lott of Wilby drives to the hoop in an NVL game against Kennedy.

second consecutive season. Coached by Marty Sparano, Kaynor also featured John DeBrito and Travis Trotman to complement the inside force of Freeman, who would be named to the CIAC Class L All-State team for a second year at season's end.

The Panthers held a 31-25 halftime lead and led Wilby by five points after three periods, before the Wildcats' pressure turned things around in the final quarter. Lott scored 21 points before fouling out late in the 60-56 victory, while Eason and Mel Burrus also reached double figures for Wilby. Freeman got his season average of 31 points and DeBrito added 12 in a losing effort for Kaynor Tech.

Wilby's come-from-behind victory was repeated days later in the showdown for the city championship against Crosby. The Bulldogs raced to a double-digit lead in the second quarter and were up by a 37-28 margin at halftime. But a trapping defense and hot shooting from Lott proved the difference after the break to secure an 82-81 win for host Wilby.

Two of the city's top performers stood out in the exciting contest played before a crowd of 1,500 at the Wildcats' gym. Crosby's Willie Davis, honored that night as 1986 recipient of the Billy Finn Award, registered 37 points and 20 rebounds. And the high-scoring sophomore Lott scored 42 points, including two free throws with four seconds left that clinched the Wilby victory.

That wouldn't be the last time Wilby and Crosby faced each other on the season, as both teams were included among the 16 squads in the West region of the CIAC Class L tournament bracket.

As top seed in the region, Wilby dispatched Whitney Tech, 57-52, in its opener while ninth-rated Crosby ran past Foran, 90-54, setting up a second-round encounter between the two city schools.

The Bulldogs started well in the state tourney showdown, with 6-7 center Davis scoring 14 points in the first quarter and junior guard Tracy Jones handling Wilby's pressure defense.

Crosby held a 43-38 lead at the break before Wilby whittled away at the lead in the second half behind the scoring of Lott and Eason – who would combine for 49 points on the night.

But the Bulldog guards provided the key plays down the stretch. Jones converted a three-point-play to tie the game at 81 with a minute and a half remaining, and Piccolo then scored the next six points to secure a 89-83 victory and a date with Warren Harding of Bridgeport in the region final.

Davis finished with 29 points, including the 1,000th point of his scholastic career, while Jones added 21 and Piccolo had 16 for Crosby. Lott matched Davis' 29 points as Wilby ended its season at 19-3.

Contributed / Crosby High School

Willie Davis, Billy Finn Award winner in 1986.

The Class L West Region final went down to the final seconds, with Harding and Crosby each having a possession with the score knotted at 57 in the final minute. The Presidents' Derek Allen proved to be the hero, converting a three-point play for the final points of the game.

Despite falling in the region final, Crosby advanced to the quarterfinals (based on the tournament format allowing each regional finalist to move on), to play a 22-1 Middletown team at Bristol Central. Behind a career-high 30 points from Piccolo, the Bulldogs enjoyed a fine shooting night in building a 20-point lead and holding on for a 83-77 victory.

The win earned Crosby a rematch with Harding in the L semifinal, but the Bulldog offense never clicked into gear as their nemesis claimed a 71-52 win at the University of New Haven. William "Frenchy" Tomlin led the way with 28 points and 10 assists for Harding, who would go on to claim a fourth consecutive CIAC title four days later.

"They seem to have a mystique over us; in my 17 years on the coaching staff here, we have not been able to beat a Harding team in the tournament," noted Crosby coach Nick Augelli in his postgame comments to the *Republican-American*.

Jones scored 20 and Davis – who would be named the Class L All-State team – had 14 for Crosby, which finished with a 16-9 record.

In the Class M tournament, both Sacred Heart and Kennedy claimed opening victories before falling to higher seeds in the second round.

The Hearts, entering the state tournament with a six-game win streak, continued their successful run by eliminating Plainville in the first round. The inside duo of Chris O'Toole and Chris Monroe combined for 39 points and Brian Murphy and Sherwin Robinson also reached double figures for 10th-seeded Sacred Heart in the 73-60 victory.

Coach Chris Murphy's Hearts then gave state power St. Joseph of Trumbull all it could handle before dropping a 83-76 decision to the second seed. The Cadets converted eight of ten free throws in the final 75 seconds of the game to hold off Sacred Heart. Brian Murphy netted 22 points, Monroe scored 17 and Kevin Mc-

Members of the *Republican-American***'s 1985-86 All-City first team included Crosby's Alan Piccolo, Tim Drakekely of Holy Cross, Crosby's Willie Davis, Phil Lott of Wilby and Kaynor Tech's Rufus Freeman.**

Carthy added 15 in the final game of the Hearts' 12-10 season.

Kennedy, seeded 13th, defeated Immaculate in its first tourney game. Mike Mallory scored 16 points and hit two free throws to break a tie with a minute left in the contest. Scott Strielkauskas, a 6--6 center, added 15 in one of his best games for the Eagles.

Down by 15 points at halftime to 5th-seeded Kolbe Cathedral in the next round, Kennedy responded with an impressive second half to force overtime before ultimately dropping a 70-68 decision. Vin Riddick notched a season-high 29 points and Mallory scored 27 as Kennedy finished with an 11-11 record.

Riddick and Mallory were named to the *Republican-American*'s All-City second team, along with Wilby's Kevin Eason and Chris O'Toole and Chris Monroe of Sacred Heart. The first team featured Willie Davis and Alan Piccolo of Crosby, Kaynor Tech's Rufus Freeman, Tim Drakeley of Holy Cross and Wilby's Phil Lott.

Davis and Lott headlined the All-NVL team, voted on by league coaches. The first team also included Holy Cross senior Drakeley, Mike Mallory of Kennedy and Torrington junior Murray Williams, who surpassed the 1,000-point plateau during the season. The All-NVL second team featured Wilson Cole of Ansonia, Watertown's Mike Svab and three city players – Eason of Wilby, Crosby's Piccolo and Monroe of Sacred Heart.

Monroe shared the Doc McInerney Award as top scholar among city seniors with Mike Gillis of Holy Cross. The year's other senior award winners were Chris O'Toole of Sacred Heart, recipient of the Lt. Jack Cullinan Award for sportsmanship, and Crosby's Davis, the Billy Finn Award winner as outstanding player.

Kaynor's History: 3 All-State performers, two undefeated regular seasons

The 1985-86 season proved historic at Kaynor Tech, with 6-5 forward/center Rufus Freeman becoming the first Panther player in school history to be named to the *New Haven Register*'s All-State team for two seasons.

Freeman, who averaged more than 30 points and 20 rebounds per game in his senior season, earned the repeat honor for Class L after leading the Panthers to the Inter-County Athletic Conference title.

Kaynor also featured John DeBrito and Travis Trotman to complement the inside force of Freeman – who was also named to the Waterbury Republican's All-City first team for his junior and senior seasons.

Contributed / Kaynor Tech High School

Kaynor Tech's Larry Dawson was named to the *New Haven Register's* Class M All-State team in 1970-71.

After high school, Freeman would move on to Mattatuck Community College, a junior-college power in the region. A two-time All-New England player at Mattatuck, he helped to lead the Chiefs to the National Junior College Basketball Tournament in Hutchinson, Kan.

He then played for Oral Roberts for two seasons, contributing to the Titans' run to the Elite Eight of the NAIA tournament in 1990.

While Freeman is the technical school's only two-time All-Stater in its history, two others earned the honor a single time. Larry Dawson was named to the Register's Class M All-State team in 1970-71, his junior year at Kaynor, while Panthers guard Chris White made the Register's Class L team as a senior in 1976-77.

White played a key role the season before, when Kaynor completed an undefeated regular season for the first time in school history. That 1975-76 squad, which also featured seniors Hank Spellman and Bob Kundrotas, advanced to the quarterfinals of the CIAC Class L tournament, losing to city foe Crosby.

That team was coached by Dick Ierardi, who was a key reserve on Wilby High's 1953 team that won a state title. Also a noted softball pitcher in area recreational leagues, Ierardi served as coach for a number of sports at Kaynor, as well as the school's athletic director, for many years.

After his passing in 2013, Kaynor Tech honored Ierardi's contributions to the school by naming the gymnasium after him.

"He brought us to another level,"

Kaynor Tech coach Dick Ierardi gives instructions to his team during a game in 1975-76, when the Panthers produced the first undefeated regular season in school history.

said Marty Sparano, who played for Ierardi and succeeded him as Kaynor's basketball coach and athletic director. "Kaynor was always the doormat that everyone loved playing. Then Dick took over, and it was tough for us to schedule games. He set the bar high," added Sparano prior to the dedication.

Sparano would guide Kaynor's basketball program until 1994, when he became director of the school's continuing education program. Spellman, a captain on the undefeated 1975-76 team, then succeeded Sparano as basketball coach at Kaynor Tech.

By the end of his first decade as coach, Spellman directed the Panthers to a second undefeated season, amid a three-year period when Kaynor compiled a 65-8 record and advanced to the quarterfinals of the state tournament each season.

The impressive run included a 20-0 regular season in 2001-02, breaking the 1976 team's 17-0 mark. Led by Dale

Saunders, Lamarr Sands and Lucas Spellman, the 2001-02 team advanced to the Connecticut Vo-Tech Conference (CVTC) tournament final – losing to Bullard-Havens of Bridgeport – and finished 23-2, setting a school record for wins in a season.

The Panther's top players would graduate, but the likes of Mantrell Gibbs and Andre Daniel stepped up from reserves to team leaders the next season to extend Kaynor Tech's successful run. Spellman's 2002-03 squad even captured the CVTC tournament to claim the school's first conference title since the Freeman years – and prove that city schools in the NVL weren't the only teams capable of producing dominant periods on the basketball court.

The Kaynor Tech program may play in the shadows of higher-profile schools in Waterbury, but the Panthers have certainly produced a storied history of their own.

1986-87: Crosby reclaims NVL title; Wilby reaches Class M semifinals

"I think we have the talent to win the league again, but we're far from a shoo-in," said Wilby coach Reggie O'Brien in his comments for the *Waterbury Republican*'s 1986-87 season preview following the city's traditional jamboree, which the Wildcats captured by outscoring Crosby 25-20 in the championship period.

"We're happy we won the jamboree, of course, but there's some hard work ahead if we're going to become the cohesive team we intend to be."

With the bulk of its regular rotation back – including the NVL's leading returning scorer in junior Phil Lott and muscular forward Kevin Eason – Wilby began as favorite to win the league in a season that saw the three-point shot first instituted by the CIAC.

All of the other city teams in the NVL featured notably different squads from the previous season. Holy Cross and Kennedy had to each replace four starters lost to graduation, while Sacred Heart had seen its two top performers from 1985-86 – Chris Monroe and Chris O'Toole – move on to college.

Crosby had lost Billy Finn Award winner Willie Davis and shooting guard Alan Piccolo to graduation, but did return three starters in Tracy Jones, Nate Ervin and Mark Ward. Coach Nick Augelli also had some experienced reserves to take on bigger roles as the Bulldogs mounted yet another challenge for top honors.

As expected, Crosby joined Wilby at the top of the NVL standings from the start, with both also collecting non-league wins in December over a Hamden team featuring the high-scoring Al Jones and future NBA player Scott Burrell.

Reprinted with permission of the Republican-American

Members of the 1986-87 All-NVL first team included, from left, Mike Mallory of Kennedy, Wilby's Kevin Eason, Murray Williams of Torrington, Wilby's Phil Lott and Shawn Watson of Crosby.

Wilby was upset by Holy Cross in early January, conceding first place in the league to cross-town rival Crosby. The Bulldogs had cruised to victory in their first six league games, with first-year starters Shawn Watson, a ballhawking guard, and 6-5 shotblocker Willie "Curt" Steward proving their worth on both sides of the ball.

The first matchup between the two schools took place at Wilby, and the home side was in command throughout to hand Crosby its first loss. Phil Lott and Kevin Eason topped 20 points apiece for Wilby, which subdued Crosby's offensive attack en route to a 96-80 win.

Guard Rob Manning and 6-1 sophomore Keith Lott, a cousin of Phil, added 18 points apiece in the Wilby win over Crosby. The two then followed that by reaching double figures in a 96-64 rout of Kennedy, and emerged as key contributors for a Wildcat team that would claim a place in the *New Haven Register*'s ranking of top ten teams in the state for the rest of the campaign.

Crosby rebounded from its subpar performance with a string of solid wins. Steward recorded a triple-double – with 21 points, 13 rebounds and 10 blocked shots – in an 85-74 triumph over Sacred Heart, before guards Tracy Jones and Watson combined for 40 points in the Bulldogs' 73-51 defeat of Holy Cross.

Wilby matched Crosby game for game as the season progressed, with Phil Lott averaging 29 points per game and Eason collecting 23 points and 13 rebounds per outing, representing the second- and third-highest scorers in the NVL behind Torrington's Murray Williams.

With the two teams holding a substantial four-game lead over third-place Sacred Heart by mid-February, the hype for a Wilby-Crosby rematch to decide the city and league champion grew by the day

Contributed / Wilby High School

Kevin Eason finishes a Wilby fastbreak with a layup during a home win.

– with one of the question marks keeping a packed house at the Crosby Palace from witnessing such a battle being an inoperable portion of the gym's bleachers that would need to be repaired in time for the season-ending contest.

Crosby had used temporary bleachers for most of the season as Nick Augelli's troops collected win after win at home. Luckily, city officials found a company to complete the mechanical work on the motorized bleachers in time.

And with the Bulldogs winning away at Ansonia while Wilby was topping Kennedy on February 27th, the stage was set: Ranked 5th and 6th in the state in the New Haven Register's Top Ten poll, 18-1 Crosby would host 18-1 Wilby in the final game of the regular season for all the marbles.

"If this isn't the biggest high school basketball game in the city ever, it certainly has to be one of the biggest," said Wilby coach Reggie O'Brien in his comments to *Waterbury Republican* reporter Roger

Cleaveland a day before the game. "It's tough to be much bigger with two 18-1 teams playing each other for two titles."

The game didn't disappoint, with each team producing some of their best basketball in a "tale of two halves" battle in front of an overflow crowd of 2,200 spectators. Kevin Eason – named the season's Billy Finn Award winner as top senior in the city that night – and Phil Lott combined for 45 points in the first half alone, and Wilby's press produced a number of turnovers as the Wildcats stormed to a 58-36 lead at halftime.

But host Crosby clamped down on defense after the break and cut away at the deficit behind strong second-half play from Shawn Watson and forward Mark Ward, who finished with 18 points and double-digit rebounds on the night.

A basket by Crosby's Mike Marshall tied the game at 82 with three-and-a-half minutes left in the fourth period, before a Ward putback gave the host Bulldogs their first lead of the night at the 2:54 mark. But Wilby didn't fold, hitting a couple of hoops in the final minute to send the game into overtime.

The back-and-forth battle continued through the extra session. Wilby's Eason hit a short jumper to put the Wildcats up 95-94 with 25 seconds left. Marshall, who had replaced the fouled-out Curt Steward midway through the fourth period, banked in a driving layup to give Crosby back the one-point advantage with nine seconds left in OT.

With plenty of time left, Wilby got off a number of shots before the final buzzer. Phil Lott missed from the right wing, but the rebound fell to Eason, whose shot was blocked by Marshall. Manning collected the ball but couldn't connect as time ran out.

Offsetting 43 points from Phil Lott and 30 from Eason, Crosby had completed a stunning second-half comeback to claim the city and NVL championships on a memorable night at The Palace. Watson led the way for the Bulldogs with 30 points; four others reached double figures, including 14 from game-winner Marshall.

"In our first game this season, we were losing to Hamden by 22 points and came back to win, so we knew we could do it," said Shawn Watson after the 96-95 win. "We put our heads up for the second half and everyone gave everything they had."

With its 19-1 record, Crosby was seeded second in the West Region of the CIAC Class L tournament, just behind a Warren Harding of Bridgeport team that was among the top 20 teams nationally in USA Today's poll.

Wilby, at 18-2, earned the number 5 seed in the West Region of the Class M tourney, and drew city rival Sacred Heart (10-9 on the season) as its first-round opponent.

A couple of other city teams collected final-week wins to earn berths into the state tournament.

Holy Cross, which had been the only team to defeat Wilby prior to Crosby's victory, won its last three games – including a 52-51 overtime decision over Wilbur Cross, the third-ranked team in the New Haven Register's Top Ten poll – to claim a place in the LL bracket. But the Crusaders' streak ended one game into the postseason; with 6-7 center Doug Leichner out sick, Holy Cross was eliminated by Stamford, 58-46, to end its season with a 10-11 record.

Kaynor Tech also garnered some late wins to make the postseason, capped by senior John DeBrito's 35-point performance as the Panthers edged Eli Whitney Tech in its regular-season finale.

The scholastic career of DeBrito, a basketball and soccer star who would go on to play professionally in Major League Soccer, would end one game later. He scored a game-high 38 points in Kaynor's 69-58 loss to Wolcott in the first round of the Class L tournament.

Crosby's journey in the L tourney began with an opening-round bye, before the Bulldogs defeated New Fairfield in the second round. Guard Tracey Jones netted 23 points while inside players Curt Steward, Mike Marshall and Nate Ervin all hit for double figures as the Bulldogs pulled away for a 91-66 victory.

That 20th win on the season would be the last for Crosby, which ran into a Cinderella team in South Catholic in the L quarterfinals. Frustrated by Catholic's slowdown game, the Bulldogs were behind 12-2 after one quarter, and a second-half comeback fell short in a 57-52 loss. Curt Steward had 16 points for Crosby, which had an off-shooting night and became the third upset victim for South Catholic, which moved on the semifinals.

Wilby may have lost the NVL title to Crosby but did advance further than the Bulldogs in state tournament play. The Wildcats stormed to a 15-2 lead over Sacred Heart in its Class M opener and cruised to a 121-82 victory. Junior star Phil Lott scored 40 points to lead five Wildcats in double-figures, while Kevin McCarthy concluded a fine scholastic career for Sacred Heart with a 22-point performance.

In the Wildcats' next outing, 32 minutes of regulation play was not enough to separate Wilby and Immaculate of Danbury.

Lott hit 18 of his game-high 31 points as Wilby claimed a 43-36 lead at the break. The advantage was up to 16 points with a minute left in the third quarter after Kevin Eason hit a pair of free throws, giving him 1,000 points for his career, But the Mustangs stormed back with a strong fourth period to send the game into overtime.

Two Immaculate free throws tied the game once more with 30 seconds left in OT, and Wilby held the ball for a final shot. Eason missed a foul-line jumper, but Lott controlled the rebound and scored with three seconds left to send Reggie O'Brien's Wildcats to the M quarterfinals.

St. Thomas Aquinas of New Britain held a double-digit lead over Wilby in the third period of that quarterfinal, but the Wildcats rallied for a 69-63 win. Rob Manning scored 16 points and Keith Lott collected 14 points and 19 rebounds as Wilby improved to 21-2.

The team standing in the way of Wilby's second appearance in a state final in five seasons was St. Joseph of Trumbull, featuring Providence-bound guard Chris Watts and 6-7 center Marvin Saddler. And while the Trumbull team controlled things most of the way, a Kevin Eason basket tied the game at 62-62 with just under four minutes to play in a physical semifinal at the Quinnipiac gym.

But the second-ranked Cadets ended the game on a 19-2 run to eliminate Wilby, with big man Saddler finishing with 27 points. Phil Lott had a team-high 21 points for the losing Wildcats and was later named to the Class M All-State team.

Wilby's 6-3 junior was also named to the All-NVL first team, along with teammate Eason. The Wilby duo was joined by Crosby's Shawn Watson, Mike Mallory of Kennedy and Torrington's Murray Williams, honored for the third straight year.

The All-NVL second team for 1986-87 featured Crosby's Curt Steward, Mike Shortell of Ansonia, Watertown's Rico Brogna, and the Sacred Heart duo of Kevin McCarthy and Brian Murphy.

The Billy Finn Award went to Kevin Eason of Wilby. Kennedy's Mike Mallory was honored with the Lt. Cullinan Award for sportsmanship and John Lawlor of Holy Cross was recipient of the Doc McInerney Award as top scholar among seniors.

Looking Back: Wilby's Phil Lott

The University of Hawaii celebrated the 100th season of its basketball program in January of 2020, and Lance Tominaga – an ESPN web editor who earned a degree in journalism from the school – recapped some of his favorite memories of Rainbow Warrior hoops for the occasion.

Among the entries in that blog post was the time Tominaga was interviewing a player before practice for a class assignment, when he heard assistant coach Bob Nash shout "We got him!" to a fellow assistant nearby – referring to a prized recruit that Hawaii was hoping to sign.

That recruit turned out to be Phil Lott, one of the best basketball players ever to come out of Waterbury, who would go on to score 1,290 points for the Rainbow Warriors and be included in another memory for Tominaga's blog – being a member of Riley Wallace's team dubbed the "Magnificent Seven" that went 25-10 and advanced to the NIT quarterfinals in 1990.

"I was being recruited by much bigger schools … Michigan, Syracuse, every Big East school except Georgetown. But like some other top players at the time, I figured that I'd at least take a recruiting visit to Hawaii," recalls Lott.

It wasn't the weather or the campus that most attracted Lott. He made a quick connection with Nash, a Hartford native who had gone on to play for (and coach) the Rainbow Warriors. "He was a big reason that I went to Hawaii," says Lott. "And he was like a father figure to me during my time there."

Apart from family, Lott considers Nash to be one of the two most influential people in his life. The other is Reggie O'Brien, who took over as coach at Wilby High during Lott's freshman season. A teacher at Wilby who was coaching the Post College basketball team, O'Brien assumed the post after Bob Freeman and assistant Dave Kalach were let go following the drowning of player Rob Donaldson in the school pool after a basketball practice in December of 1984.

Devastated by the loss of a teammate, the Wildcat team was also suspended for a month and a half by city school officials, denied the start of their season until late January and forfeiting nearly half of the scheduled games that season.

Lott himself had endured a more personal loss a few months earlier, when his mother died during the summer before his freshman year at Wilby. He credits his sisters with guiding him through some tough times while his scholastic basketball career began to take shape under the mentorship of a new coach.

"Reggie really helped me in so many ways, and he showed me the way, in basketball and in life," says Lott. "From an urging to stay away from negative things and make the right choices, to harping on us to eat right, he showed he really cared. And it wasn't just for me … he truly cared for every player he coached."

When the Wildcats were finally allowed to play that season, freshman Lott was in the starting lineup alongside two sophomores against Torrington. After that initial road loss, Lott scored 30 points and the young Wilby side defeated Sacred Heart, 86-84, for its first win of the 1984-85 season.

The next season, with O'Brien coaching at Post and Wilby, Lott and junior Kevin Eason shouldered the scoring load for the Wildcats – who captured the 1985-

86 NVL title by overtaking Crosby late in the season.

The title clincher came in dramatic fashion in a game against Kennedy, who had played a deliberate style to keep the score low. But it was Wilby that held the ball for an extended final possession, and a jumper from the 6-4 Lott fell through the net as the buzzer sounded to give the Wildcats the victory and the school a first league crown in 12 years.

"Some people may have been surprised that such a young team claimed the title, but as players we didn't think of our age compared to our opponents, we just went out and played things one game at a time," notes Lott, who credits the play of 5-3 guard Ted Mcintosh on both ends of the floor as a major factor in Wilby's success that season.

The NVL title came down to one-game scenarios the next two seasons – with Wilby involved in both – as Lott would become one of only a handful of players to be named to the All-NVL first team for three seasons.

Phil's cousin Keith Lott and Rob Manning had emerged as key contributors for the 1986-87 Wilby team, which took an 18-1 record into the final regular season game at Crosby. But the Bulldogs, also 18-1 and also ranked among the top ten teams in the state, were looking to avenge their only loss of the season in a showdown that O'Brien called "one of the biggest games in city history" in a preview article appearing in the *Waterbury Republican.*

Phil Lott was inducted into the New Haven Tap-Off Club's Hall of Fame at a November 2019 ceremony.

Lott and Eason combined for 45 first-half points as Wilby took a 20-point lead to halftime, only for a second-half rally by Crosby send the game to overtime. Down by one point with ten seconds left in overtime, Lott and Eason had shot attempts miss the mark. Crosby escaped with a 96-95 victory – and the NVL title – offsetting a game-high 43 points from Lott.

"Sometimes it is the losses that you remember most, and that was one of the most memorable games of my high school career," recalls Lott. "We had a big lead but then began to miss some shots and make some turnovers. It was like a domino effect and eventually the tide turned in Crosby's favor."

Wilby also lost a one-game NVL playoff to Holy Cross in 1987-88, Lott's senior season that saw him top 50 points on four occasions. The three-point shot had been instituted the season before, and Lott's deep shooting range proved that much more beneficial in combining with his physical presence to overcome opposing defenses.

Choosing a memorable contest from that final season, Lott recalls the night he set the city's modern-day single-game scoring mark against Kennedy. Coming one week after Crosby's Wayne Boyette had poured in 59 points against Sacred Heart, Lott felt the scoring touch from the start, converting 23 field goals and ending with 60 points in a 107-80 home win.

The effort was also noteworthy as the total meant that Lott had surpassed 2,000 points for his high school career – making him the first player in city history (and seventh in the state) to reach that mark.

Wilby would end the season with a CIAC tournament loss to St. Bernard, having reached a CIAC semifinal and a quarterfinal during Lott's time there. "People forget I was the tallest player on the team, and we struggled when facing teams with some real height," notes Lott, who was named All-State for a second consecutive season and ended his career with 2,230 points – third highest in state history at the time.

Besides all the points and wins in high school, it is the kinship developed with teammates that has meant the most to Lott, along with the unforgettable bond he established with Coach O'Brien. "I remember that Reg had bought a new car before our prom. And he let me take that car to the prom, while his own son took the older car," quips Lott, who even had O'Brien visit a number of times in Hawaii.

The Wilby star maintained a close relationship with his high school coach until O'Brien's passing following a heart attack in 2002. Lott was among the former Wildcats who played a role in a 2003 ceremony dedicating the school gym in O'Brien's name.

After his outstanding college career at Hawaii, Lott spent a decade playing professionally in Europe and Israel before returning home to Waterbury. "In those first few years in Europe, I wondered why my older teammates would always be complaining about sore knees, backs or feet every night," recalls Lott. "But it wasn't too long that I started experiencing the same aches and pains, and I called it a career after around ten years or so."

Lott has spent a number of years working in the Waterbury school system since then; he is now a truancy prevention specialist. He coached the Crosby girls basketball team before stepping aside in 2019 to watch his two sons, Zion and Zaire, make their way through their middle school and high school basketball years.

Zion Lott followed in his father' footsteps by being named recipient of the Billy Finn award for the 2020-21 season, 23 years after Phil earned the honor.

Phil also has coached Zion's age-group team through the AAU ranks — from when they were 7-and 8-year-olds to now, nearly college level. "We have had a great group of kids stay together since those early years, and a couple have Division I potential," says Lott. "It has been great to see them grow, and to have the chance to pass along some of the same guidance and wisdom that Coach Nash and Coach OBrien imparted on me."

1987-88: Crusaders win CIAC title as McDonald and Lott eras end

Waterbury sports fans were treated to another thrilling high school basketball season in 1987-88, which featured a one-game playoff between two city teams for the Naugatuck Valley League title and a first-ever state title for one of those schools.

Taking advantage of the three-point shot – instituted for CIAC games one year earlier – three different players topped the single-game individual scoring record set in 1961 by the legendary Billy Finn. And the season marked the end of an era for both a player and coach who would go down as legends in city lore.

Wilby returned the league's top scorer in 6-4 All-State swingman Phil Lott from a team that reached the Class M semifinals. Cousin Keith Lott, a 6-1 junior, was also back, but Reggie O'Brien's Wildcats had lost three starters to graduation that included 1987 Billy Finn Award winner Kevin Eason.

Defending champion Crosby, which had topped Wilby in overtime in the final game of the regular season to claim the previous year's NVL crown, also had to replace some key starters – but featured a strong front line in 6-6 Curt Steward, 6-5 Mark Ward and Mike Marshall.

The two public schools were among the main contenders in 1987-88, along with a deep, experienced Holy Cross team aiming for a first league title since 1981. The Crusaders had gone 10-10 the previous year, but returned nearly their full squad led by seniors LaMarr "Dewey" Stinson, Doug Leichner and Tony Santos.

The 6-3 Stinson announced before the season that he had signed to play college basketball at Fordham University. Another pre-season announcement came out of Holy Cross, with long-time coach Tim McDonald deciding the season would be his last at the helm of the Crusader program.

Aiming to send McDonald off with a successful season, Holy Cross started its league campaign well with wins over both main rivals. The 6-7 Leichner scored 32 points and Stinson added 25 to lead the Crusaders past Wilby, 78-71, in double overtime on January 5th at The Pit.

The victory earned Holy Cross the early lead in the NVL standings. And with senior Dyran Henderson and junior guard Wesley Oates emerging as key contributors as the season wore on, McDonald's squad maintained the slim margin at the top.

Wilby kept pace behind Phil Lott, who would seemingly set another city scoring record each time he stepped on the floor during the 1987-88 season. The University of Hawaii-bound forward surpassed the 50-point mark twice in the Wildcats' first four games – first tying the modern-day city single-game record with 52 points against Kaynor Tech and then scorching the nets for 59 points, including nine three-pointers, in a rout of Sacred Heart.

Averaging 34 points a game on the season, Lott would go on to break the single-season scoring total set by Spencer Harrison of Holy Cross in 1979.

With Keith Jordan and Brandon Sumler settling in to the guard spots in Wilby's lineup and Dwayne Ellis adding a boost off the bench, the Wildcats gained steam

Contributed / Wilby High School

Phil Lott of Wilby drives to the hoop for two of the 2,230 points of his high school career.

with a series of wins leading up to the rematch with Holy Cross.

In that Feb. 5th encounter, host Wilby claimed an early lead and then held off a Holy Cross rally to pull away for an 83-73 victory. Keith Lott played a strong game with 21 points and 14 rebounds, and cousin Phil scored 29 as the Wildcats evened things at the top of the NVL standings. Stinson matched Lott's 29 points and Oates hit for 25 in the Crusaders' first loss in the league.

The result left the two teams tied at the top of the league standings, with a handful of games remaining to determine an NVL champion.

Holy Cross responded by routing Crosby, 85-58, in one its best performances of the season. Stinson's 23 points led four double-figure scorers in the Crusaders'

home win, while junior Wayne Boyette netted 24 points for Crosby – one game after he scored 59 in a 109-85 win over Sacred Heart.

Lott outdid Boyette by one point in Wilby's 107-80 home win over Kennedy, a game where he became the first player in city history to surpass 2,000 points in his career. The Wildcats sprinted to a 25-point lead by halftime, turning the contest into a shootout with Lott aiming for the record books. The 6-4 senior hit 23 field goals on the way to his 60 points, setting the modern-day single-game scoring mark and becoming just the seventh player in state history to reach 2,000 points in a scholastic career.

With the final night of the regular season requiring both Wilby and Holy Cross to win to set up a one-game playoff for the NVL title, the Crusaders had the easier assignment. Tim McDonald's squad had the upper hand from the opening tip against Sacred Heart and cruised to a 104-86 victory. Dewey Stinson – who in pre-game ceremonies was awarded the Lt. Jack Cullinan Award for sportsmanship among city seniors – scored 34 points and Wes Oates added 23 for Holy Cross, which finished the regular season with a 17-3 record (17-1 in the NVL).

Wilby had a tougher task in its traditional season-ender against Crosby, and the dramatic back-and-forth battle went down to the final seconds. The Bulldogs went into the final period with the lead and were up by two points with a minute remaining.

Phil Lott, who had an off shooting night, then hit his only three pointer to put Wilby up 79-78. After Crosby's Wayne Boyette hit one of two free throws tie the game, the ball was back in Wilby's possession with time running down. With most in the crowd expecting Lott to take the deciding shot, the 6-4 senior

Members of the *Republican-American's* 1987-88 All-City first team included, from left, Derreck Pruden of Sacred Heart, Kennedy's LaMarr Powell, Dewey Stinson of Holy Cross, Crosby's Wayne Boyette and Phil Lott of Wilby.

found Dwayne Ellis in the lane for a lay-up with seven seconds remaining for the game's final points.

Boyette, who equalled Lott's 33 point-effort on the night, got off a shot at the buzzer but could not connect, giving Wilby the victory and setting up the playoff showdown with Holy Cross for the league crown.

In that title decider played at Crosby High, the Crusaders used a 29-9 first-half run to take command by the intermission. But Phil and Keith Lott led a Wilby surge that cut the lead to three points midway through the fourth period.

With the game and the NVL title in the balance, Holy Cross' Stinson stepped up with six straight points – including a thunderous dunk on a fast break – to build the lead to 75-66 with two minutes remaining and essentially seal the victory.

The Fordham-bound Stinson finished with 27 points while Leichner scored 22, converting five of seven free throws in the final period, in the 85-77 win. Phil Lott had a game-high 36 points for Wilby, which lost the title decider for a second season in a row after capturing the NVL crown in 1985-86.

Despite the loss, the 19-2 Wildcats were ranked second in the Class L tournament, and first in the West Region of the bracket, as one of three city teams (along with Kennedy and Sacred Heart) in that division.

The Hearts, the 11th seed, held their own against Bassick of Bridgeport in the first half of an opening-round contest, before falling 90-80 to the sixth-seeded Lions. Brian Murphy collected 18 points and 10 rebounds for Sacred Heart alongside three other senior classmates – Darren Evans, Derreck Pruden and Steve Hebb – who all hit double figures in the last games of their scholastic careers for the Hearts, who finished 10-11.

Kennedy also lost in the first round, dropping a 41-40 decision to a taller Seymour side. Al Gonzalez and LaMarr Powell had ten points apiece for the Eagles, who ended the season with a 12-9 record.

That result kept two city teams from playing in the second round, as Wilby awaited the victor. But Seymour was no match for Phil Lott and the Wildcats in a game played at Naugatuck High. Wilby scored 37 points in the third period en route to a 102-65 second-round win, with Lott notching 26 points to break the city's single-season scoring record of 798 points (that was set in 1979 by Spencer Harrison of Holy Cross).

Two nights after setting that mark, Phil Lott's scholastic career would come to an end when Wilby fell to 10th-seeded St. Bernard in the Class L quarterfinals.

The Wildcats struggled throughout, and were behind by ten points on two occasions before battling back to take a four-point lead with a minute remaining. But the Saints' defense forced a couple of turnovers and Will Flowers made some key buckets in the closing minute to complete the upset over Wilby.

Lott scored 21 – to end his career with 2,230 points, third most in state history at the time – while Keith Jordan and Keith Lott also reached double figures in the loss as Wilby finished the season with a 21-3 record.

**Holy Cross coach
Tim McDonald**

That left Holy Cross as the lone city team remaining in state tournament brackets. The Crusaders, ranked third in the Class LL division, had held off New Canaan, 63-52, in its opener and defeated Wilton, 89-65, in the second round. Strong shooting nights from Wes Oates, who hit four three-pointers among his 24 points, and Dyran Henderson (22 points) sparked the Crusader win over Wilton, which had upset Crosby in an opening-round game.

Holy Cross ran into a hot shooter in the next round but survived the quarterfinal affair against East Hartford. The Hornets' Troy McKoy hit seven threes and scored 52 points, but the Crusaders converted 26 of 32 foul shots on the night to secure a 79-76 victory and extend the coaching career of Tim McDonald.

The Class LL semifinal against an upstart Hartford Bulkeley team was a tight, deliberately paced affair for most of the game. Up by three points after three periods, Holy Cross scored 12 of the game's next 14 points to pull away for a 50-37 victory, with seniors Stinson and Leichner combining for 32 points.

That meant that McDonald's final game at the helm would come in a state final, the third time he had guided the Crusaders to the LL title game – having lost to Wilbur Cross in 1981 and to Norwalk in 1982.

Norwalk would represent the opponent again this time; the Bears held an identical record to Holy Cross (22-3) and featured a strong inside game led by 6-9 center Todd Holland.

The Fairfield-bound Holland picked up two first-quarter fouls in the final, yet Norwalk maintained a 35-34 advantage at halftime. Stinson then scored seven points and the 6-7 Leichner added five in a third quarter that saw Holy Cross retake the lead.

The back-and-forth affair was tied twice in a dramatic final period, the last at 57-all with three-and-a-half minutes remaining. Stinson then gave Holy Cross the lead with one of his patented spinning drives to the hoop, and converted the ensuing foul shot for a crucial three-point play.

Holland and Leichner traded baskets before Norwalk's big man fouled out with two minutes to play, having scored 20 points.

Norwalk cut the lead to 64-63 with under a minute left, but Crusader reserve guard Mike Kolesnik scored on a drive with 35 seconds left – for his only points of the game – and Dyran Henderson and Tony

Santos each sank two free throws to secure a 70-65 Holy Cross victory and the first state basketball title in school history.

Stinson, who finished with 21 points and 15 rebounds, was named the game's most valuable player. Leichner, Henderson and Wes Oates also hit double figures for the victorious Crusaders in Coach McDonald's final game on the sidelines.

"He is so much more than a coach," Leichner said of McDonald to reporters after the game. "He is a model for us all and we wanted very much to win this for him, as well as ourselves."

"It's a great feeling," acknowledged McDonald, head coach since Holy Cross first started a varsity program in 1970-71. "But this championship is not just for me but for all 1,500 students in the school."

McDonald, who would continue to serve Holy Cross students in administrative positions through the 2014-15 school year, finished his 18-year coaching career with 279 wins and seven Naugatuck Valley League titles.

Stinson and Wilby's Phil Lott, who ended his career as the Naugatuck Valley League's all-time leading scorer, were named first-team All-State for their respective classes by the *New Haven Register*. The two also headed the 1987-88 All-NVL team, with Lott becoming just the sixth player to be named All-NVL for three seasons.

Also selected to the All-NVL team were the Crosby pair of Wayne Boyette and Curt Steward and Sacred Heart's Derreck Pruden – who joined Lott and Boyette in surpassing the decades-old single-game scoring mark when he hit for 54 points in a win over Naugatuck.

Contributed / Wilby High School

Dewey Stinson of Holy Cross attempts to block a shot put up by Wilby's Dwayne Ellis in a game at Wilby during the 1987-88 season.

Stinson and Lott also headlined the All-City team announced by the *Republican-American*. The first team also included Boyette of Crosby, Sacred Heart's Pruden, and LaMarr Powell of Kennedy.

The Holy Cross pair of Doug Leichner and Wes Oates made the All-City second team, joined by Curt Steward of Crosby, Wilby's Keith Lott and Brian Murphy of Sacred Heart.

Winners of the city's annual awards for seniors included Phil Lott as the 1988 recipient of the Billy Finn Award. Stinson of Holy Cross was honored with the city's sportsmanship award, named in honor of Lt. Jack Cullinan, and Sacred Heart's Steve Hebb earned the Doc McInerney Award as top scholar among the year's seniors.

Looking back: Dewey Stinson Recalls Holy Cross' championship season

The 1987-88 Holy Cross basketball team made history by defeating Norwalk in the Class LL title game, becoming the first state champion in any sport in the school's history.

Coming in Coach Tim McDonald's final year at the helm of the Crusaders' hoop program, the accomplishment was that much more satisfying for a team that persevered through some adversity – and a 10-10 regular season one year earlier – to produce the storybook ending.

"Going into our senior year, we believed we had a chance to be good, but there was definitely pressure as we hadn't had success to that point," says Dewey Stinson, one of the team captains in 1987-88. "The prior year we struggled and underachieved, I think, in most folks' eyes … in a very good league with quality teams throughout."

During the summer between his junior and senior seasons, the Crusaders participated in a team camp at Wake Forest University. "That experience was huge for us, as we got a chance to compete against some very tough teams and we had a very good showing," recalls Stinson.

The trip provided a confidence boost for the Crusader players, who "then had an added all-or-nothing mentality once Coach Mac announced (during the preseason) that it would be his final year," believes Stinson. "Being one of the most selfless men ever, Coach never made it about him. But it was hard not to feel that needed to send him off in a successful way."

Led by a solid group of seniors – Stinson, 6-7 center Doug Leichner, point guard Tony Santos and versatile Dyran Henderson – Holy Cross started the league season well, with early wins over main rivals Wilby and Crosby.

A February defeat to Wilby and its star Phil Lott was the Crusaders' lone loss in the NVL. A one-game playoff between the two city teams was needed to determine the NVL champion. Stinson scored six straight points in the closing minutes of a tight contest to lead Holy Cross to a 75-66 victory and give McDonald an NVL crown in his final year as coach.

The Crusaders then rode their momentum into the state tournament, winning their next five game to claim the CIAC Class LL crown. The 6-3 Stinson collected 21 points and 15 rebounds in the championship game win over Norwalk, to earn most valuable players honors in the title game.

Stinson went on to play college basketball at Fordham University, and happened to face another Waterburian in the NCAA tournament when the Rams qualified for the Big Dance in his senior season.

"Fordham was in the MAAC (Metro Atlantic Athletic Conference) my freshman and sophomore seasons, and we faced some tough LaSalle teams that had a number of future NBA players (Lionel Simmons, Randy Woods, Tim Legler), and we ended up in the NIT."

The Rams then joined a new conference, the Patriot League, for Stinson's junior season. "We had the second longest win streak (to UNLV) that year, and beat several teams that made the tournament. But we were snubbed by the NCAA for at at-large bid, and lost in a play-in game for the tourney (being in a brand new conference)."

Fordham finally made the tournament in Stinson's senior season, but lost to a UMass team that included Jerome Malloy, who starred at Kennedy and was the Billy Finn Award winner in 1991.

Thirty years on from that game, Stinson

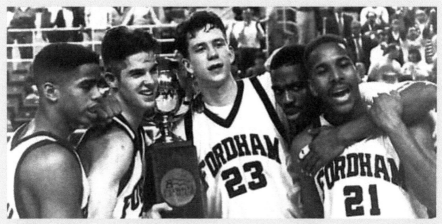

Dewey Stinson, far right, celebrates a Patriot League title with his Fordham team-mates in 1991.

lives in the New York City area with his two daughters, ages 12 and 13. "And I have had the good fortune of working in the sports media industry over the last 20-plus years," adds Stinson, who has fond memories of his final year of high school basketball.

Besides the state championship game, the most memorable games that senior year for Stinson were the matchups with Wilby and an early-season encounter with state power Warren Harding of Bridgeport.

"Any time you get to play against argu-ably the city's greatest player ever in Phil Lott, it was special, and – with the league playoff – we got to face Wilby three times my senior season," notes Stinson. "Phil was like LeBron – on the court, he was smarter, stronger, more skilled and athletic than anyone out there."

Games between Holy Cross and Wilby during Stinson's years "were always tight, yet that senior year we were on a mission and able to take two out of the three and win the league."

Another highlight came in the Crusad-ers' second game of the season, in the Pearl Street Holiday Festival at Kennedy's gym, against Warren Harding of Bridge-port – which was ranked number one in the state, and also included in USA

Today's Top 20 national ranking of teams.

"We had a lead for most of the game. At some point in the fourth quarter we were up a few baskets, before we literally threw the game away with three back-to-back turnovers," says Stinson. "And to my amazement I remember them going into a stall. I guess it was a smart tactic, but un-expected when you have this uber-talent-ed team trying to survive in that manner. I also remember this game as I missed key free throws late in the game... Ughhh!"

That game may have ended in defeat but did help to show the Crusaders they could compete with the best teams in the state. By season's end, the confidence and experience gained over the years paid off, along with the guidance of McDonald, who was "super-prepared, disciplined and knowledgeable," remembers Stinson.

"He was more than a coach, educator, and teacher … he was a father figure to so many, to many that sorely lacked that type of influence in their life," says Stinson. "He was an authoritarian, with a golden heart."

McDonald's "announcement (to retire) was hard to believe at the time, recalls Stinson, "but it gave us some additional motivation, if we needed it. It obviously made the whole year that much more special; it was a fairy tale."

1988-89: Powell, Malloy lead Kennedy to league championship

The 1988-89 high school season brought a former coach back to the boys basketball scene in Waterbury, with Ed Generali taking over as Holy Cross coach following the retirement of Tim McDonald.

Generali had guided Sacred Heart to the CIAC Class M title in 1984, and had coached the Crusaders girls team for the previous three seasons, leading the team to a 1988 state final.

With many key players having graduated from Holy Cross' state-title winning team, Generali inherited a young squad in his initial season. His first win as Holy Cross coach came in the Crusaders' third game of the season. Wes Oates led the way with 21 points in a 85-69 decision over Wolcott.

With Holy Cross in somewhat of a re-building mode, the city's three public schools proved to be the main contenders for city and Naugatuck Valley League championships.

Crosby's Wayne Boyette, considered the top returning player on the season, assumed much of the scoring load for Nick Augelli's Bulldogs – who lost most of their starting frontline to graduation but would include 6-6 sophomores Harun Ramey and Ryan Sullivan in the rotation.

Kennedy had some talented sophomores of its own. Jerome Malloy and Malik Williams were primed for bigger roles to complement seniors LaMarr Powell and Alberto Gonzalez as coach Jack Taglia's Eagles looked sure to improve on the 12-9 record from 1987-88.

Wilby had to replace just one starter, but that was one mighty hole to fill as Phil Lott had taken his city- and NVL-record 2,230 points to the University of Hawaii. Keith Lott, Brandon Sumler and Dwayne Ellis were back for Reggie O'Brien's team, who began the season with a favorable early schedule.

Wilby won its first five league contests before being upset in a road game at Naugatuck. Greyhound guard Eric Mudry converted a three-point play with nine seconds left to provide the winning margin in a 68-65 thriller. Rob Plasky led Naugatuck with a game-high 26 points, while junior Anthony Banks scored 17 points and Keith Lott added 13 for Wilby.

Kennedy toppled Sacred Heart, 75-66, on the same night to improve to 7-0 and assume top spot on its own in the NVL standings. Malloy, Powell and Gonzalez – who hit five three-pointers – all topped 20 points in the win.

The eventful evening also saw Boyette of Crosby score 49 points and beat the buzzer with a tip-in of a missed shot to beat Holy Cross, 85-84. Mike Phelan's two free throws had given Holy Cross a one-point lead with ten seconds remaining before Boyette, who recorded 22 points in the fourth quarter, rescued the Bulldogs.

Crosby followed that with another dramatic win that went down to the final buzzer. Boyette netted 32 points and guard Derrick Copeland scored the Bulldogs' final four points in an 83-81 decision at Wilby, which wasn't secured until Anthony Banks' potential game-winning three-pointer for the hosts bounded off the rim as the horn sounded.

That result moved Crosby above Wilby into second place with a 7-1 league re-

1988-89 NVL champion Kennedy Eagles

cord, the Bulldogs' lone loss being an 58-55 defeat to leaders Kennedy.

Malik Williams had suffered a broken hand in that early Kennedy win over Crosby, limiting the Eagles' depth in the frontcourt as the season wore on.

Kennedy coped well without Williams, but his absence was evident when the Eagles visited Wilby. The host Wildcats surged to a 20-point lead by halftime and held on for an 83-70 victory. Keith Lott collected 23 points and 17 rebounds and Dwayne contributed 21 points as Wilby knocked Kennedy from the unbeaten ranks.

With the potential for a three-way tie (among the city's public schools) looming, an early February battle between Crosby and Kennedy proved pivotal at the top of the league standings. With 6-3 senior Wayne Boyette on his way to a 35-point night, the Bulldogs looked to be in control, ahead by double digits in the third period. But Kennedy rallied behind some some sharp shooting from distance to claim a 78-76 victory. LaMarr Powell net-

ted 33 points and four Eagles combined to hit seven treys as Coach Taglia's men regained the top spot in the standings.

Kennedy then maneuvered through games against Sacred Heart and Holy Cross to move closer to a first league title since 1972. Entering the final week of NVL play, the 16-1 Eagles hosted 14-2 Wilby with a chance to clinch the league title.

The visiting Wildcats had the upper hand early and took a 29-20 halftime lead to the locker room. A couple of Kennedy runs cut into the lead, but Wilby maintained a 56-50 lead with three minutes remaining in the game.

Jerome Malloy, the sweet-shooting sophomore who would finish with a game-high 30 points, hit a jumper and LaMarr Powell hit three of four free throws to cut the deficit to one point as Kennedy continued to whittle away at the lead.

Two trips down the court for Wilby produced missed shots, and then Alberto Gonzalez hit a shot from the lane to give Kennedy a 57-56 lead. Wilby could not counter with a bucket, allowing Powell to seal the 59-56 victory with two more free throws.

The home fans filled the court to celebrate Kennedy's rally to claim city and NVL crowns, both firsts for Coach Taglia – who hailed the late offensive surge but credited his team's defense for the win.

"We played the best man-to-man defense we've played in years, holding Wilby to nine fourth-quarter points," noted Taglia to *Waterbury Republican* reporters after the game. "What more fitting way could we have done it than to beat the only team that beat us, in front of our home crowd?"

Kennedy's stellar season earned the team the second seed – and an opening-round bye – in the Class L tournament. while Wilby settled for the 10th seed in the same division.

Two other city teams qualified for the postseason, with both positioned in the Class LL tournament. Crosby ended its regular season with a 95-92 win over Wilby – with Wayne Boyette pouring in 48 points on the night he was honored with the Billy Finn Award – and was selected as the seventh seed in LL. And Holy Cross finished with a 10-10 record to earn a CIAC berth in Ed Generali's first season as coach.

Kennedy coach Jack Taglia

The 25th-seeded Crusaders travelled to Westhill of Stamford for its opener. Rodney Spann connected on ten three-pointers for eighth-seeded Westhill, who advanced with a comfortable 81-64 triumph. Senior guard Mike Kolesnik scored 24 points in his final game for a Holy Cross team that gained some postseason experience that would prove beneficial in future seasons.

Crosby needed a strong second half to advance past Staples of Westport in its first-round encounter. Sophomore center Ryan Sullivan scored 21 points in his best performance of the year for the Bulldogs, and classmate Harun Ramey contributed 13 points and 16 rebounds in the Bulldogs' win.

Two nights later, Crosby dropped a 98-82 decision to a Wilton team that shot 60 percent from the field. Boyette scored 34 points and Antwon Wright added 12 in their final games in a Crosby uniform, on a night that would see Waterbury's three remaining teams all eliminated from CIAC play.

Wilby had routed East Catholic in the first round, with Keith Lott surpassing 1,000 points for his scholastic career. But the Wildcats ran into hot-shooting Matt Curtis of Cheshire, who notched a school-record 44 points to lead the Rams to an 86-69 victory that ended the Wildcats' season at 16-6.

Kennedy also saw its season end on March 9, falling to 15th-seeded St. Bernard of Montville by a 60-59 scoreline. There were ten lead changes in the fourth quarter of the L quarterfinal, until a pair of free throws by Rusty Ellington with 20 seconds left gave the visitors the upset victory. Jerome Malloy scored 20 points while senior Alberto Gonzalez added 19 for Kennedy.

Two of Kennedy's leaders – Malloy and LaMarr Powell – were named to the *Waterbury Republican*'s All-City and All-NVL teams, which featured identical first teamers for just the second time in the 45 years that the squads had been selected.

Others chosen for the teams included Keith Lott of Wilby, Sacred Heart guard Jay Maia and Wayne Boyette of Crosby, who led the league in scoring.

Looking Back: Kennedy's Taglia details Eagles' consecutive championships

Approaching the end of his first ten years as head basketball coach at Kennedy in the late 1980s, Jack Taglia remembers that he had "begun to seriously question whether I would ever get the opportunity to contend for a league championship as a coach."

In taking over from Marty Sweeney prior to the 1977-78 season, Taglia's Eagles had proved competitive but couldn't secure a Naugatuck Valley League title during his initial decade at the helm.

"In the mid-1980s we had a couple of good years. We won 17 games one year with guys like Vern Riddick, Neil Ware, and Bill Evans. However there was always one or two teams we couldn't get by," recalls Taglia.

Kennedy's 1988-89 team – led by forward LaMarr Powell, point guard Alberto Gonzalez and sophomore swingman Jerome Malloy – would not only change the coach's mindset but start a run of three consecutive NVL titles for Kennedy – a feat that hadn't been achieved by a league school in more than 50 years.

The Eagles started out with seven straight wins before losing to Wilby in January of 1989. "But the team recovered well, and went on another winning streak. It was then I began to realize that we had something real," notes Taglia.

Kennedy was 18-1 going into its last game of the regular season. In order to capture a first Naugatuck Valley League title for Taglia, the Eagles had to avenge their only loss against Wilby in a game that would decide the league championship.

"To this day, I can still feel the electricity. The gym was a madhouse; its maximum seating was around 1545, but I know we had more than that amount of people packed in to the gym on that night," says Taglia.

The game went down to the wire, with Malloy scoring 30 points and leading a second-half Kennedy comeback. Down by a point in the final minute, Gonzalez hit a short jumper to give the Eagles a 57-56 lead. After Wilby could not convert on its next possession, Powell hit two free throws to seal the result, giving Taglia his first league title as coach.

"The place went berserk. Our student body and our fans were on cloud nine," says Taglia. "I remember just sitting on the scorer's table watching the players being mobbed, and how excited and relieved our fans were that we finally reached the top of the mountain."

Powell and Gonzalez would graduate, but Kennedy had "good players in the pipeline for the next couple of years," notes Taglia. The smooth-shooting Malloy was among a number of key players returning for 1989-90, including Malik Williams – who was lost to injury midway through the previous season – and Garnett Petteway.

The three were joined by point guard Waverly Battle and the versatile Mike Byrd, "who hit two amazing, last-second shots to win games that season," recalls Taglia. "The first was from the top of the key off of a broken out-of-bounds play to beat Holy Cross at the buzzer and propel us to a second league championship."

Byrd's second buzzer-beater came with Kennedy trailing St. Thomas Aquinas by two points in a Class M semifinal at Plainville High. The half-court attempt banked in with no time left on the clock, completing an overtime rally that put the Eagles into the state championship game.

"The CIAC tournament is really no different than the NCAA tournament in that you are always going to have at least one nail-biter game and you need a little luck," believes Taglia. "We had both of those in our run to the finals in 1990."

Top seed and defending champion New London proved too much in the M final, defeating Kennedy 64-56. With two players 6-8 or taller, "their front line dwarfed ours and we were not small," notes Taglia. "They out-rebounded us and had too many second attempts. That combination is hard to overcome."

The 6-3 Malloy was phenomenal in defeat, registering 32 points and 16 rebounds against New London. "He was heads and shoulders above everyone on the court that day. He showed the entire state what kind of a player he was," adds Taglia, noting that the 6-3 junior was named most valuable player of the game despite being on the losing side.

"I had said earlier that at one point I never thought we'd win a league championship. Well, a state championship game is something you only see in dreams," says Taglia. "I had chills when I turned toward the crowd behind us that day and saw what seemed like half of Waterbury, including the mayor, cheering us on," recalls Taglia. "It was a moment in coaching that I will never forget."

Malloy would surpass 2,000 career points the next season, in what many consider to be one of the most competitive seasons in city and NVL history. All five Waterbury schools were in contention for the 1990-91 league title, before

Kennedy and Wilby finished tied atop the NVL standings.

The two met in a one-game playoff at Crosby, where seniors Malloy and Williams combined for 69 points to lead the Eagles to a third consecutive NVL championship. Williams hit two free throws with 28 seconds remaining to give Kennedy the lead for good and reach the 1,000-point plateau for his career.

So, in a period of a few years, the coach who had doubted if he'd ever claim an NVL title had become the first coach to lead his team to three straight league championships in over half a century.

"There was no doubt we had great players," says Taglia, "but they were dedicated, committed and had a work ethic that in my estimation no one could duplicate."

From the start of his coaching career, Taglia realized that he had to put in the work to become successful.

"Just because you bounced a ball, it doesn't mean that you can coach the game. I had a lot to learn," recalls Taglia, who was substitute teaching at Kennedy while going to graduate school when Marty Sweeney asked if he'd be interested in helping out the freshman team in the 1972-73 season.

A couple of years later, Taglia was a varsity assistant to Sweeney, "who was the type of coach who visualized the game two or three plays ahead," says Taglia. "He knew his opponents' weaknesses and in practice always worked to take advantage of them. He was not only one of the better players to come out of Waterbury, but he brought that knowledge of the game to the Kennedy team."

Once Taglia took over the head coaching role, he found himself going against his own high school coach – John Gilmore of Sacred Heart – for a couple of seasons.

"When he retired I did ask him a lot about his philosophy, what he taught, and how he practiced," remembers Taglia. "What I learned from John was the effort needed to understand the game, the hard work needed to be successful and how to prepare for each season,"

Taglia and Gilmore went to a lot of clinics together. "We saw, along with Ed Generali, all of the best college coaches in the country at one time or another. Today coaches just go to the internet. Back then we had to travel to see theses guys," Taglia quipped.

The two have remained close friends after their coaching careers ended. "I always admired John as a coach and a gentleman," says Taglia. "He was the classic definition of a student of the game. He really knew how to coach the game."

One of the college coaches Taglia tried to emulate was Dean Smith of North Carolina. "I would videotape Carolina's games on TV, and I bought his book, which was a textbook on his entire program, and I went to see him in person on two occasions," recalls the former Kennedy coach.

"The longer I coached, the more I realized that playing good defense is so important to the success of your program, says Taglia. "To the day I retired, I used all of Coach Smith's breakdown drills every day in practice, and I committed myself to trying to be the best man-to-man team we could be."

As Taglia gained more coaching experience, his approach to the game and his coaching philosophy came more into focus. "I learned a lot from the people I surrounded myself with and they taught me there was no substitute for hard work and dedication," he adds. "I tried to instill this same work ethic in my players. They never let me down."

That was never more evident in Kennedy's run of three straight Naugatuck Valley League championships. "But the one thing I will always remember is there were no easy games in the league during that time, especially the city teams," says Taglia. "We had some battles every night and these guys always rose to the occasion."

While those title-winning seasons were the most memorable for Taglia, the former Kennedy coach never questioned the hard work and effort his players put into the program.

"When you're limping into the final week of the season with no chance of making the tournament it's easy to quit, miss practice and put your head down," adds Taglia. "I can honestly say that my players respected the game and always gave their best effort up to the final buzzer of the season.

"For that I'll alway be indebted to them. In my 31 years as head coach every one of my guys were responsible, dedicated and of the highest integrity. I have the utmost respect for every one of them."

Contributed / Kennedy High School

Coach Jack Taglia directs a Kennedy practice at the school gym.

1989-90: Byrd's buzzer-beaters fuel Kennedy's run to Class M final

An eventful decade of Waterbury basketball would come to a close with the 1989-90 high school season, with many fans in the city once again wondering if they would see a repeat NVL champion for the first time since the 1976-77 season.

Defending champ Kennedy High, led by Jerome Malloy and Malik Williams, certainly had the necessary components in place to complete the task. But realizing the fierce spirit of competition among city schools, most followers wouldn't discount the chance that a different squad captured the crown – all while expecting some pleasant surprises to emerge throughout the campaign.

One such surprise for the 1989-90 season was a Holy Cross team without any returning stars that finished 10-11 the previous season. Ed Generali's Crusaders relied on its frontcourt depth and a talented backcourt of Rob Paternostro and Matt Mariani to battle for city and NVL titles.

Holy Cross started the season with an impressive winning streak. And when the Crusaders hosted Kennedy in a January 19 encounter, both sides took identical 7-0 league records into the game.

The defending NVL champions led by double digits in the third period, before the hosts mounted a comeback to prevail, 95-91, in a high-paced affair. Rob Paternostro led Holy Cross' balanced attack with 26 points while Scott Mandy, Tom McDermott, Chris Hamel and Bob Lasbury also hit for double figures. Jerome Malloy netted 36 points for Kennedy in its first loss of the campaign.

The Crusaders' win streak continued until a matchup with Wilby on February 2. Reggie O'Brien's Wildcats produced a strong performance to claim a 95-87 victory to end Holy Cross' run at 12 games.

Kennedy – which edged Sacred Heart that same night to again claim a share of the lead in the NVL standings – had kept pace all season with arguably its strongest team during coach Jack Taglia's tenure. Malloy, who had already surpassed 1,000 points for his career, and Williams were the high scorers; forward Garnett Petteway had emerged as the top sophomore in the city; and Waverly Battle, Mike Byrd and Trevor Morris played key roles on both sides of the ball.

With a rematch against Holy Cross in their sights, the high-flying Eagles continued to roll with wins against a couple of suburban opponents – highlighted by a 34-point rout of Wolcott when Malloy and Williams combined for 48 points.

But the upstart Crusaders held strong as well, evidenced by a 107-81 romp over Crosby to move to 15-1 in the league. Sharpshooter Matt Mariani hit eight three-pointers and scored 30 points while Rob Paternostro had 29 in the impressive win over a Bulldog team that lost two guards midway through the campaign.

The loss in personnel affected Crosby's performances on the season, leaving a focus on the frontcourt – where another of the season's surprises emerged in 6-6 junior Harun Ramey. He had impressed during his sophomore season but took his game to another level in 1989-90 to match Malloy as one of the top players in the league and in the state.

The left-handed Ramey averaged 29 points, 15 rebounds and four blocked shots per game on the season. He topped 30 points a number of games, scored 41 against Naugatuck and poured in a city- and NVL-record 68 points in a rout of Wolcott on February 13.

Wilby's Anthony Banks and Brendan McCarthy of Sacred Heart also stood out as some of the top individual scorers in the NVL, but the team title would come down to the Holy Cross-Kennedy re- match at the Eagles' gymnasium.

The sellout crowd was treated to a game fitting of a championship contest that featured nine ties, nine lead changes and an overtime period. And the game seemed headed for another extra period after Tom McDermott blocked a Kennedy shot out of bounds with two sec- onds left in overtime.

Kennedy players were slow to come back onto the court fol- lowing a time-out to set up a last-second attempt. With the referee having already begun the five-second count by the time inbounder Malik Williams got to the ball, the planned play turned into a scramble. Williams found Mike Byrd near the top of the key, and the senior guard had enough time to release a shot from behind the arc before the buzzer sounded. The ball dropped through the net, and Kennedy had avenged its only loss of the season. Malloy and Williams combined for 40 points in the Eagles' 65-62 victory, while Holy Cross was led by by big man Tom McDermott's 21 points, along with 16 from Matt Mariani.

Kennedy still needed to defeat

a solid Naugatuck team three days later to clinch a second consecutive NVL title. Taglia's men stuck to business and pulled away for a 92-73 win. Malloy and Naugy big man Allen McLain shared top-scor- ing honors with 37 points each, and sophomore Garnett Petteway scored 27 for the victors.

Other final-night contests included an impressive performance by Wilby, which had eight players score in double figures in a 102-95 defeat of Crosby. Cazzie Iver- son and Andre Stevenson each had 20 points while Anthony Banks, who was honored with the Billy Finn Award after

Contributed / Kennedy High School

Kennedy's Jerome Malloy, the all-time leading scorer in school history, in action against Wilby.

the game as top senior player in the city, scored 14 points for the Wildcats.

Kennedy led a contingent of six city schools into the CIAC tournament, including a Kaynor Tech team that qualified in the last week of its regular season. The Panthers dropped their Class L opener, 64-50 to St. Bernard, with Jason Arnauckas finishing off a fine individual season with 19 points in the loss,

Three other teams from Waterbury also lost in the first round. Sacred Heart stayed with seventh-seeded Kolbe-Cathedral of Bridgeport for one half of its Class M opener, before dropping a 91-78 decision to end its season at 10-11. Wilby, ranked sixth in Class M, endured a cold-shooting night and fell to Bristol Eastern, 70-62.

In Class L, Crosby fell behind early at home to Darien and could not recover. A hot-shooting Paul Fiorita hit eight three-pointers and scored 38 points for Darien in the 82-65 upset win; Harun Ramey hit for 33 points and Ryan Sullivan contributed 10 for the Bulldogs, who ended the campaign at 13-8.

Kennedy and Holy Cross, the top two finishers in the league, fared better in their CIAC openers – and each would make deep runs in their respective brackets.

Holy Cross, seeded fifth in Class LL, hosted a Rockville team with a formidable frontline in the first round. The visitors were able to play to a 30-30 tie as the first half ended, before the Crusader guards took control. Rob Paternostro and Matt Mariani – who hit five three-pointers – combined for 51 points as Holy Cross pulled away for a 83-62 victory.

Mariani scored 20 points in the next round, with Holy Cross escaping with a 66-64 win over Southington. The Crusaders had built up a ten-point lead, but

a basket from 6-6 Kris Steele gave Southington a one-point lead with three minutes to play in the fourth period. Mariani responded with a pair of late treys, and Scott Mandy's key steal and layup in the closing seconds helped seal the win as Holy Cross improved to 19-3 on the season.

Win number 20 came in easier fashion for Coach Ed Generali's Crusaders, who dominated the second half to defeat Shelton by a 105-77 scoreline. Big man Tom McDermott produced a career-high 25 points and grabbed 17 rebounds for Holy Cross, which received 27 points from Paternostro and 14 from forward Chris Hamel in the quarterfinal victory.

Up next for the Crusaders was Wilbur Cross of New Haven, which had battled Holy Cross in a number of memorable tournament games in the early 1980s. The eight-seeded Governors' uptempo pace took its toll on Holy Cross in the LL semifinal, and an 11-0 Wilbur Cross run over the second and third periods proved too tough to overcome.

Paternostro netted 18 points and McDermott scored 16 for Holy Cross, which finished with a 20-4 record and a state semifinal appearance in Generali's second season at the helm.

Kennedy's journey in the Class M tournament began with a home game against Immaculate of Danbury. The Mustangs played a deliberate style that slowed Kennedy for the first 10 minutes. But the second-seeded Eagles picked up the pace with some aggressive defense to build a double-digit lead by halftime and cruise to a 71-52 home victory, its 20th win of the season.

The Eagles fast-paced transition game kicked into gear against Haddam Killingworth in the second round. Jerome Malloy poured in 37 points and Malik Williams, Waverly Battle and Garnett Petteway all hit double figures in the

81-52 victory, sending Kennedy into the quarterfinals against Kolbe-Cathedral.

Down by nine points to Kolbe with two-and-a-half minutes left in the game, Kennedy staged a dramatic comeback to send the game into overtime, capped by a Malik Williams' three-pointer with 20 seconds left. And with Kolbe's high-scorer Lyle Jones having fouled out, Kennedy controlled the overtime session to prevail, 76-69.

"When you win games like this, you think maybe Lady Luck is on your side," stated coach Jack Taglia after the game. And that post-game quote for the *Waterbury Republican* was reinforced in Kennedy's next game, when Mike Byrd banked in a 30-footer – his second buzzer-beating trey of the season – to defeat St. Thomas Aquinas, 56-55, in the semifinals.

Each team had chances to win in regulation, but missed fouls shots on both ends sent the game to overtime. Aquinas then grabbed a four-point lead in the final minute of OT, before Malik Williams scored to cut the deficit to 55-53. Saints' star Scott Sytulek then missed again from the foul line, giving Kennedy the ball with seven seconds left.

Byrd was forced to dribble out wide as the clock ticked down, but he had enough time to release a shot from distance – and play the buzzer-beating hero once again – ending third-seeded Aquinas' season at 23-3.

Kennedy had reached its first-ever CIAC state final, with top seed and defending champion New London – featuring 6-8 Matt Rollins and 6-9 Pete Gittens – presenting a sizable title-game opponent.

The smaller Eagles held their own on the backboards but their shooting proved lacking in the championship game.

Gittens, who scored 19 points on the night, helped stake New London to a six-point halftime lead.

Jerome Malloy led a Kennedy comeback after the break, but the experienced Whalers – with four players in double figures – held on for a 64-56 win. Malloy had an exceptional night, collecting 32 points and 16 rebounds, and was named the game's most valuable player – a rare feat for a player from the losing side in a title game.

Malloy – who would be named to the Class M All-State team – and Kennedy teammate Williams headed the *Republican*'s All-City first team. Finn Award winner Anthony Banks of Wilby was also selected, along with Crosby's Harun Ramey and Rob Paternostro of Holy Cross.

Two Sacred Heart players – Brendan McCarthy and Jason Dorso – were named to the All-City second team, which also included Kennedy's Garnett Petteway, Matt Mariani of Holy Cross, and Wilby's Cazzie Iverson.

Contributed / Crosby High School

Crosby coach Nick Augelli congratulates Harun Ramey after the junior forward broke the city's single-game scoring mark with a 68-point effort against Wolcott.

Looking Back: Kennedy's Malik Williams

If there was one member of the Kennedy High basketball team most satisfied with the team repeating as Naugatuck Valley League champions in the 1989-90 season, it was junior forward Malik Williams.

"I felt like I had let my team down the previous year – even though we were able to win that first NVL title – because I had broken my right wrist in a game against Crosby and missed a key part of the season," says Williams.

"It was a low point for me personally. But I was able to develop my left hand while recovering," remembers Williams. "And then I went to Five Star camp and joined Wayne Simone's Connecticut Select AAU program in the summer months and we travelled throughout the country playing top talent."

Confident that he had put in the work to further his game, Williams was "chomping at the bit to make an impact as we defended the NVL title."

Kennedy would not only claim another league trophy but advance all the way to the Class M final in the 1990 state tournament.

Williams was named to the *Republican*'s All-City team and played a key role in two comeback victories during the Eagles' postseason run. His three-pointer sent the quarterfinal against Kolbe-Cathedral into overtime, where Kennedy pulled away for a 76-69 win.

The Eagles next game also went to overtime. Trailing St. Thomas Aquinas by four points in the final minute of the extra period, Williams hit a basket to halve the deficit before teammate Mike Byrd banked in a three-pointer to send Kennedy into the Class M championship game.

"That season showed me that hard work determination and desire will push you to the limits," says Williams. "Although we came up short in the state final, it was a thrill."

Williams and classmate Jerome Malloy would then repeat as first-team All-City selections their senior season, when Kennedy made history by becoming the first NVL school in 50 years to win three straight league titles.

The Eagles needed to beat Wilby in a one-game playoff for the NVL crown that 1990-91 season, another dramatic affair that went down to the closing seconds. Williams scored 30 points in the 93-89 victory; his two free throws with 28 seconds remaining in the game gave Kennedy the lead for good – and gave the 6-4 forward 1,000 points for his career.

After coming up short of qualifying academically, Williams headed to Oxnard College in California, averaging ten points a game his freshman season. But the injury bug would strike again, as a torn ACL sustained during the off-season sidelined the Kennedy graduate.

As so many players have learned, the ACL is such a difficult injury to return from. Williams ended up transferring to the University of Bridgeport and then California State Stanislaus during his time at the next level.

"At CSU Stanislaus, the school and the coach were at odds. It was all politics in that situation. Basketball was not the same for me at that point," says Williams. "I finished the season, graduated and started working with a non-profit in Stockton, California, assisting people with special needs and disabilities. I found my path finding and coordinating services for this population."

In 2005, Williams began coaching basketball at Edison High in Stockton, and now coaches at Cesar Chavez High, under head coach Harris, in the same town. Williams also is head coach for both the boys and girls' golf teams at the school.

" I was introduced to the sport by a friend about 20 years ago," notes Williams, and instantly fell in love with the game and its principles."

Malik and wife Renee have two children – Vanessa, 25, Jalen, 18 – and a grandchild, Olive, who just turned 6. Family plays a big role in life for Williams, who considers his mother Gloria Clarke the biggest influence in his life.

"She loves her family and her community, and retired from the state of Connecticut in 2015 after 30 years of service," notes Williams. "She filled me with a belief that with hard work and dedication, everything is possible."

That mindset and family-type environment was reinforced during his high school days, evidenced by the bonds he made with teammates. "Kennedy players and teams were a close unit during my time. We spent a tremendous amount of time together," remembers Williams.

Upper-class students and former players played a big role in the development of players coming into the Kennedy program, according to Williams. "Freshman year was a learning experience for me. Coach Taglia was loyal to his seniors and upperclassmen," he adds. "I understand now why he did that; so that the young guys can learn from the veterans and do what is expected and then pass it along."

Contributed / Chavez High School

Malik Williams, back center, with the boys basketball team at Cesar Chavez High School in Stockton, California.

Williams is appreciative of the life lessons learned during his high school years. "The Kennedy faculty was attentive and caring. And I was able to build lifelong bonds with the folks I met during my time there. Huge influences from Mike Mallory, Neil Ware, Chris Love and countless other who impacted my development."

The love of competition and "drive to want to be the best were certainly motivators for those teams under Coach Taglia," notes Williams. "Also the ability to sacrifice was a big part of being successful."

Proud to be a part of the group of players who carried that tradition from the 1980s into the '90s, Williams remembers that "we stuck together for a common goal; we were responsible to each other. We are brothers for life.

"And, you know, winning is contagious; you want to keep winning," he adds. "That has seemed to translate in my life; I really feel like a winner, and I got that from my time at Kennedy."

Selecting a 'High Five' for the 1980s

With the second ten-year period covered, it is time to pause and consider an All-Star team for the 1980s, using the restrictions required when selecting a "High Five" for the '70s earlier in the book.

Allowed to choose just one player per city high school while choosing a two-guard, two-forward, one-center lineup, here is an offering for a "High Five" of Waterbury high school basketball for the 1980s.

■ Phil Lott, 1988 Wilby graduate is first on the team sheet as one of the forwards. The first player from the city to surpass 2,000 points for his career, Lott helped to lead Wilby to the Naugatuck Valley League title in 1985-86, his sophomore season.

Lott, one of a few city players to be named to the All-NVL first team for three seasons, went on to play at the University of Hawaii.

■ Kelly Monroe of Holy Cross is another to be named All-NVL for three seasons, and gets the nod as small forward for this All-Star squad of the 1980s.

Named the Billy Finn Award winner for the 1984-85 season, Monroe graduated as the leading scorer in school history with 1,447 points.

Monroe signed to play for Boston College in the Big East then transferred to Manhattan after two seasons. He averaged 17 points per game in 1988-89, the fifth highest scoring average in the Metro Atlantic Athletic Conference that year.

■ Filling the center position is Willie Davis of Crosby, who helped lead the Bulldogs to the 1984-85 league title and an appearance in the Class L semifinals in 1985-86. A two-time All-NVL performer, Davis was recipient of the Billy Finn Award in 1985-86,

In college, Big Will was an NAIA All-American at Alderson Broaddus in West Virginia. He went on to play professionally in Europe and was a teammate of Lott's when the two were in Austria.

■ As one of the smoothest shooters in the city's history, Jerome Malloy is the choice for one of the guard positions for the 1980s' team. The left-hander from Kennedy played into the 1990-91 season but had massive contributions for the Eagles' consecutive NL championships to end the 1980s.

Malloy averaged 29 points per game and 14 rebounds for both his junior and senior seasons, and left school as the second player in Waterbury to surpass 2,000 points. The two-time All-State pick holds the unusual distinction of being named the MVP of the 1990 Class M state championship tournament, even though the Eagles were runner-up to New London in the title game that season.

The 6-3 Malloy played for two NCAA tournament teams at the University of Massachusetts before transferring to Jacksonville, where he averaged double figures and led the Sun Belt conference in three-point field goal shooting percentage for the 1994-95 season.

■ The other guard spot goes to Anthony Perry of Sacred Heart, the only player on this All-Star to team to win a state championship.

Perry surpassed 1,000 points for his scholastic career in the 1984 Class M championship game, when he scored 23 points in the Hearts' victory over Weston to earn most valuable player honors.

A two-time All-City selection, Perry was named recipient of the Billy Finn Award as top senior player in the city for the 1983-84 season.

■ As a sixth man for this "High Five" for the 1980s, Rufus Freeman produced some impressive numbers during his time at Kaynor Tech. The 6-5 forward-center averaged 30 points his senior season, when he led the Panthers to Inter-County Athletic League title.

A two-time All-State player, Freeman was an All-New England performer while at Mattatuck Community College before enrolling at Oral Roberts University to finish his college career.

'Hooparazzi' happy snapping today's stars

Contributed

From left, Clay Johnson, Simon Manning, Rob Nunley and Derek Ward.

City basketball fans are likley to see at least one of these men at a high school game these days. These former city hoopsters now prefer to take their shots from the sidelines, capturing game action involving high schoolers of the 2000s with their cameras.

Clay Johnson, Holy Cross star from the 1970s; Derek Ward, a member of Crosby's team that appeared in the 1982 Class L final, and Simon Manning, who played for Wilby, are just a few of the talented photographers whose images can be found on social media sites, helping to highlight the younger generation's achievements.

Thanks to the growing crop of 'hooparazzi' for your contributions to Waterbury's hoop scene!

The 1990s

Manny Wright of Wilby tries to get a shot off against Malik Williams of Kennedy during the playoff game to decide the 1990-91 Naugatuck Valley League championship. Kennedy was the victor, 93-89, to claim a third straight NVL title.

1990-91: Kennedy three-peats as city stakes claim as best in state

"For State's Finest Basketball, Look No Further Than Waterbury" was the headline topping the *Hartford Courant*'s scholastic basketball season preview section in its December 9, 1990 edition.

The lead article by staff writer Woody Anderson described the five city high schools that play in the Naugatuck Valley League as the "Fearsome Five," while a listing of the top players in Connecticut for the upcoming season included five players from Waterbury among the top 20 in the state – including Jerome Malloy of Kennedy at number two and Crosby's Harun Ramey at number three.

Six more players from Waterbury schools were included among 30 names comprising "honorable mention" players for the season in the state. And the *Courant*'s ranking of "top 15 sophomores to watch" featured four players from the Brass City.

"Unequivocally, Waterbury has the best talent in New England," remarked Steve Gibbs, director of the Hoop Mountain basketball camp in Northfield, Massachusetts, in the article. "Over the past five years, you could see the upsurge."

The claim was echoed by Naugatuck High's coach Joe Distasio, also quoted in the article. "There are more good players in Waterbury than ever," said DiStasio. "They (the five teams) all return their best players.

Wayne Simone, coach of the Connecticut Select AAU team who regularly took top players from the Northeast all over the country to compete in summer tournaments, added: "Before, I had to go to Danbury, Hartford, Springfield and Atlantic City for players. Now I can just go to Waterbury and be just as competitive."

Tempering some of the praise, Wilby coach Reggie O'Brien noted, "We have a very good crop of players this year. But I don't know if you can say we are better than New Haven or Bridgeport."

No matter the verdict, Waterbury was gaining in stature among the top hoop hot beds in the state as the 1990s dawned. New Haven, Bridgeport and Hartford could certainly still lay claim to some of the best basketball in Connecticut, but the Brass City had joined the state's elite – and had its talent spread among more high schools than the other cities.

Each of those high schools in Waterbury had high hopes going into the 1990-91 Naugatuck Valley League season, which looked to be one of the best ever in the its history. And it did not disappoint.

Kennedy High was looking for a third consecutive NVL title. Coach Jack Taglia's Eagles featured the aforementioned Malloy, an All-State swingman, along with 6-4 senior Malik Williams and 6-2 junior Garnett Petteway. Both were also included in the *Courant*'s top 20 players in the state. Having reached the Class M title game the previous season, Kennedy would have to find a replacement for departed point guard Waverly Battle as it defended its crown.

Holy Cross, NVL runner-up in 1989-90, featured one of the best point guards in the league in 6-0 senior Rob Paternostro. Fellow seniors Matt Mariani and 6-5 center Tom McDermott were also back, but Ed Generali's Crusaders had lost some key frontline performers to graduation.

The versatile Brendan McCarthy, rated as the 17th-best player in the state in the *Hartford Courant*'s preseason rankings, was one of three starters returning for Sacred Heart. Willie Wilson, Daryl Brown and Larry Pierce were other senior leaders for Coach Chris Murphy's Hearts, who were sure to improve on a 12-9 record in the previous season.

Wilby featured a quick, young squad aiming to return to the top of the league, after finishing second in the NVL standings three of the previous four years. Junior guard Manny Wright and sophomores Terrence Lott and Marcus Robinson were primed for increased roles in Coach Reggie O'Brien's rotation, playing alongside seniors George Hurdle, Ron Draper and 6-7 center Adam Leach.

Harun Ramey – the 6-6 forward who had already committed to play his college basketball at St. Peter's – was back for his senior season at Crosby, winner of the preseason city jamboree. The Bulldogs' frontcourt also featured 6-7 senior Ryan Sullivan, but Nick Augelli's backcourt lacked some experienced leaders as the season began.

Results during the first month of the campaign revealed how competitively balanced the city teams were. In a game one week before Christmas, Wilby outlasted Kennedy, with Marcus Robinson – who scored 19 points – and Ron Draper converting free throws in the final seconds to seal a home 66-63 win for the Wildcats.

Sacred Heart also produced an impressive, early-season victory, handing Holy Cross what would be its worst loss of the season, 85-65. The Crusaders responded

by topping Wilby – 86-73, behind Matt Mariani's eight three-pointers – and then trouncing Crosby, 98-79, with Rob Paternostro scoring 40 points and hitting all 22 of his shots from the foul line in the home win.

Wilby rebounded from that setback by dealing Sacred Heart a 84-72 defeat. Manny Wright and Marcus Robinson combined for 42 points, offsetting Willie Wilson's 32 points for the Hearts. The win moved the Wildcats to 5-1 in the league, to share the NVL lead with Crosby and Holy Cross at that point in the season.

Kennedy began to recover from a slow start and some cancellations by racing past Holy Cross, 82-69, sparked by a 21-1 scoring run in the second quarter. Jerome Malloy (32 points, 18 rebounds and 10 assists) and Malik Williams (22 points, 17 points and 10 assists) each collected a triple double to pace the Eagles. Paternostro hit for 19 points and sophomore Brian Davis notched 13 points and 15 rebounds for the Crusaders.

Wilby and Crosby, both sporting 6-1 league records, met for the first time on the season on January 22. The Bulldogs built an early lead on the strength of its strong frontline, but then succumbed to the host Wildcats' pressing, scrambling style of play. Sophomore Marcus Robinson scored 23 points and Ron Draper contributed 19 for Wilby while Harun Ramey had a game-high 28 points for Crosby.

Two nights later, Wilby travelled to Kennedy for one of the more dramatic contests of the season. The first period belonged to Wilby, which used a full-court trapping defense and a 13-0 spurt to take a 25-11 lead. But Kennedy soon settled itself behind Malloy, Williams and the rebounding of Trevor Morris to claim a one-point advantage at halftime.

The lead changed hands numerous

Members of the *Waterbury Republican*'s 1990-91 All-City and All-NVL first teams included Sacred Heart's Brendan McCarthy, Jerome Malloy and Malik Williams of Kennedy, Crosby's Harun Ramey and Rob Paternostro of Holy Cross.

times during the second half, with the Wildcats ahead by one point in the final minute. Holding possession for a final shot, Kennedy worked the ball to Malloy, who scored off a rebound of his own miss with one second remaining to give the host Eagles an 83-82 victory. Malik Williams poured in 36 points and Malloy collected his second triple double in three games as Kennedy avenged its only loss of the season. Robinson and Adam Leach each scored 19 for Wilby.

League standings at that point of the season indicated how tight things were at the top, with each of the five city teams in with a chance for a league title.

NVL standings on January 25:

Team	League	Overall
Kennedy	6-1	7-1
Holy Cross	7-2	8-2
Wilby	7-2	8-2
Crosby	6-2	7-3
Sacred Heart	5-2	5-4

The month of February began with a pair of crucial contests between city teams on the same night. Sacred Heart put together one of its best performances of the season to knock off Kennedy, 88-83. Brendan McCarthy hit five three-pointers and netted 24 points to lead five Hearts players in double figures, while Malloy and Williams combined for 56 points in a losing effort.

That same night, Holy Cross held off a late Wilby rally to defeat the Wildcats for a second time on the season. Paternostro hit for 35 points and reserve Tom Santopietro scored some key late baskets in the 80-73 victory, which lifted the Crusaders to the top of the league standings.

Kennedy clicked back into gear the following week, defeating Crosby twice to signal its intent on another NVL title. Malloy, Williams and Garnett Petteway all surpassed 20 points and the Eagles defense forced 18 turnovers in a 92-77 home win over the Bulldogs (in a makeup of a January postponement). Four nights later, the 6-3 Malloy poured in 35 points in the Eagles' 95-90 win at the Crosby Palace Harun Ramey produced another fine outing by scoring 38 points for the Bulldogs, who dropped to 10-4 in league games.

The twists and turns among city teams continued with a battle between the city's Catholic high schools. Sacred Heart opened with a hot-shooting first half, and topped the century mark in a 106-95 win at Holy Cross. Willie Wilson's 25 points paced five Hearts in double figures in a fast-paced game that saw the teams combine for 20 three-pointers. Paternostro and 6-5 Tom McDermott combined for 51 points for Holy Cross, which dropped half a game behind Kennedy at the top of the league standings.

Contributed

After playing professionally in England and Belgium, Holy Cross grad Rob Paternostro has coached the Leicester Riders to multiple championships in the British Basketball League.

A week later, Holy Cross's title hopes were dealt another blow after Harun Ramey led Crosby to an 88-78 win over the Crusaders. With teammate Ryan Sullivan out, the 6-6 senior showed why he was one of the top players in the state, collecting 35 points, 18 rebounds and six blocked shots in the Bulldogs' home victory. Shawn McCarvell added a season-high 23 points for Crosby to help offset the 46 points from the Holy Cross backcourt of Rob Paternostro and Matt Mariani.

Across town that night, Wilby outran Sacred Heart, 87-77, to move to 13-3 in league games. Terrance Lott's 19 points and Manny Wright's 18 paced the Wildcats, while Brendan McCarthy netted 29 points for the Hearts.

Wright hit for 20 points in Wilby's next game, a 78-62 win at Watertown that enabled the Wildcats to take over first place in the NVL standings. It was made possible by another result that night, as Holy

NVL standings on February 9:		
Team	League	Overall
Kennedy	11-2	12-2
Holy Cross	11-3	12-3
Wilby	11-3	12-3
Sacred Heart	9-3	9-5
Crosby	10-4	11-5

Cross' slowdown strategy paid off in 51-48 decision over Kennedy. Sticking to a deliberate offensive game plan after establishing an early lead, the Crusaders held off an Eagles rally and converted late foul shots to claim a crucial home victory.

Amazingly, the NVL standings on February 21 showed just a game and a half separating the five city schools at the top of the league. And based on the teams' remaining schedules, there existed a scenario in which the "Fearsome Five" would all finish tied for the lead at the end of the regular season.

NVL standings on February 21:

Team	League	Overall
Wilby	14-3	15-3
Kennedy	13-3	15-3
Crosby	13-4	14-5
Holy Cross	13-4	14-4
Sacred Heart	12-4	12-6

A result the next evening made the five-way deadlock impossible. Wilby rallied past Crosby, 84-80, on the Bulldogs' home court to clinch at least a share of the NVL title.

The hosts were ahead by ten points midway through the third period when Harun Ramey picked up his fourth foul. Wilby used its pressure defense to surge ahead by the start of the fourth period, which would see eight lead changes before the Wildcats took the lead for good at 73-72.

Manny Wright led a balanced Wilby attack with 20 points while Ramey scored 24 and Ryan Sullivan had 23 for Crosby, which finished the league season at 13-5.

Kennedy topped Naugatuck the same night and then defeated Sacred Heart in its next game, 92-75 – to set up a one-game playoff with Wilby to determine the 1991 NVL champion. The smooth-shooting Jerome Malloy made history against the Hearts, becoming the second player in city and league history to surpass 2,000 points for his career.

Wilby and Kennedy had split a pair of close contests games in the regular season, and the NVL playoff on a neutral court at the Crosby Palace was not settled until the final seconds.

Wilby may have lacked the experience and overall size of its opponent but led most of the way in the title tilt, and was ahead by seven points with four minutes left in the game. Kennedy's senior stars Malloy and Williams made some key hoops down the stretch to level the score at 89-89 in the final minute.

Williams then hit two free throws with 28 seconds remaining – reaching the 1,000-point plateau for his high school career – to give the Eagles the lead. A scramble for a loose ball on Wilby's next possession went the way of Kennedy at the ten-second mark, and a Malloy hoop sealed the result, 93-89, giving the Eagles another NVL title.

Malloy finished with a season-high 39 points and Williams had 30, while Garnett Petteway and Trevor Morris contributed double-figure rebounds for the victors. Junior guard Manny Wright scored 27 points for Wilby, while Marcus Robinson added 19.

"We thought we had it. But we made some mistakes near the end and they capitalized on them. That's where the experience paid off," Wright said after the game to the *Waterbury Republican*'s Pat Drewry, who likened the game to an Ali-Frazier heavyweight fight.

"Wilby is a real good team and you can't count them out until the final second. But we wanted it real bad. Even being down by seven, we knew we could come back," said Kennedy's Malik Williams to reporters after the game. "It was the best win ever. It was a win for history."

History indeed, as Kennedy became the first school to win three straight Naugatuck Valley League titles in 56 years (after Bridgeport Central accomplished the feat in the conference's first decade of play, from 1933 to 1935).

The 1990-91 NVL season, arguably the most competitive campaign in league annals, proved historic in another sense. It marked the first time in the conference's history that the Waterbury schools did not lose a single game against suburban schools. City teams had been dominating in titles won for a few decades, but the combined 50-0 record represented the first city sweep in NVL contests over a full season.

Waterbury's "Fearsome Five" had dealt each other punch after punch over a season-long fight for the league title, which left each team bruised at points but certainly battle-hardened for the state tournament. The question remained: would such a physically and emotionally draining season hamper any runs for CIAC glory?

One of the five squads felt the effects physically. Crosby's second-leading scorer Ryan Sullivan tore a knee ligament in the team's first postseason practice. With the 6-7 center done for the season, the Bulldogs advanced past Fairfield Prep in its Class LL opener but were eliminated by Bridgeport Central in the second round. Harun Ramey scored 30 points in his final high school game as Crosby ended the season at 15-5.

Reprinted with permission of the Republican-American

Garnett Petteway puts up a shot as Adam Leach of Wilby defends during the 1990-91 NVL playoff game won by Kennedy at the Crosby gym.

Holy Cross, Waterbury's other entry in the Class LL bracket, opened with an 80-64 victory over Hamden. Matt Mariani's 16 points led four players in double figures, with Tom McDermott and Brian Davis also grabbing ten-plus rebounds in the home win.

The Crusaders' second-round game – a rematch of the previous year's semifinal against Wilbur Cross of New Haven – went down to the final seconds before it was decided. Each team had a possession with the score knotted at 61 in the last minute. Wilbur Cross turned the ball over, before Crusader guard Rob Paternostro drove the lane and hit a shot with four seconds remaining to send Holy Cross on the quarterfinals. The winning bucket represented points 999 and 1,000 in Paternostro's high school career, and avenged a defeat to the New Haven school one year earlier.

Paternostro scored 36 points in the quarterfinal, but a bigger Stamford Westhill side controlled the boards and outlasted Holy Cross, 91-79, to end the Crusaders' season at 18-5.

Like Crosby, Kennedy began its postseason short of one starter (after receiving a first-round bye). A flu bug kept junior Garnett Petteway out of the Eagles' Class M game against Kolbe-Cathedral, and Kennedy found itself trailing by three points entering the final period.

Garnett's younger brother Garrett hit a three-pointer to tie the game and spark a Kennedy comeback. With Malik Williams in foul trouble, Jerome Malloy took on more of the scoring load and ended with a season-high 41 points in the 87-79 home win.

Petteway was back for the quarterfinal against Notre Dame of Fairfield, scoring 16 points for host Kennedy, which used a 10-0 third-quarter spurt to pull away for a 89-78 victory.

Up next in the M semifinals was St. Thomas Aquinas of New Britain, who had eliminated Sacred Heart one round earlier. The Hearts' fine season included two wins in the CIAC tournament, including a 63-53 defeat of two-time defending champion New London.

The Aquinas-Kennedy semifinal was a rematch of the previous year's encounter at the same stage, when Mike Byrd's three-pointer beat the buzzer to send Kennedy to its lone appearance in a CIAC final. The result of the rematch was decided well before the final buzzer; Aquinas relied on its height advantage and a triangle-and-two defense to limit Malloy and Williams and claim a 71-59 decision.

Wilby provided Waterbury with another representative in a CIAC semifinal after a deep run in the Class L division. The Wildcats' postseason began with a 87-61 defeat of league foe Naugatuck, with Manny Wright and Terrence Lott each topping 20 points. Wilby fell behind early to Bethel in the second round, but recovered with a strong second half to move on via a 81-63 scoreline.

With Wright not playing in the quarterfinals (due to illness), Ron Draper took full advantage of a rare starting opportunity and scored 34 points to lead Wilby past Ridgefield, 85-76.

The Wildcats then started slow in the semifinal against a Warren Harding team aiming for an eighth appearance in a state final in nine years. Harding's aggressive press produced an early advantage, and the Bridgeport team cruised to a 76-63 victory. Sophomores Marcus Robinson (21 points) and Terrence Lott (11) were high scorers for Wilby, which ended the season with a 20-5 record.

Waterbury may not have produced a state champion in the 1990-91 basketball season, but the epic league season and four teams reaching CIAC quarterfinals or semifinals was an indication that the city could hold its own against squads from New Haven and Bridgeport.

Kennedy's Jerome Malloy received the Billy Finn Award as top senior player in the city, while Harun Ramey was named recipient of the Lt. Jack Cullinan Award for sportsmanship among city seniors.

Both were repeat selections to *New Haven Register*'s All-State team and headlined both the *Waterbury Republican*'s All-City and All-NVL teams, which featured an identical five players. Along with Malloy and Ramey, the teams included Rob Paternostro of Holy Cross, Kennedy's Malik Williams of Kennedy, and Brendan McCarthy of Sacred Heart.

Looking back on the 1990-91 season: 'Each game felt like a championship'

"The first thing that comes to mind when I think back on the 1990-91 basketball season is just how good each of the city teams were," says Ryan Sullivan, a senior forward/center at Crosby High that season.

Each team was composed of "a core of really talented players," continues Sullivan, who paired with Harun Ramey – ranked third-best player in the state by the *Hartford Courant* – in Crosby's frontcourt.

Kennedy featured Jerome Malloy, Malik Williams and Garnett Petteway, all listed

Contributed / Holy Cross High School

Matt Mariani of Holy Cross looks for a teammate while being guarded by Adam Leach in a 1991 home game against Wilby.

within the top 13 slots on the *Courant's* ranking of top players in Connecticut that season. Sacred Heart had its own top-20 player in Brendan McCarthy, along with Willie Wilson and Daryl Brown.

Rob Paternostro, the best point guard in the league, teamed with deep shooting threat Matt Mariani and big man Tom McDermott at Holy Cross, while Wilby featured future All-State performers in Manny Wright and Marcus Robinson.

"That year marked the first time that the city teams went undefeated (50-0) against the so-called 'suburban teams' of the NVL," notes Sullivan, "which meant that each and every city game was going to be important, and you better bring your 'A' game if you were hoping to win. City gyms were packed. Each and every game was a dogfight."

"It was an exciting time, for sure," says former Holy Cross guard Matt Mariani, who considers both the 1989-90 and 1990-91 seasons as especially competitive among the talented city teams.

"Every city game, plus games against Torrington, were tough in both of those seasons. There were no easy outs," says Mariani. "The gyms were always loud and full of great energy, and any team could win on any given night."

Holy Cross' 1989-90 team was a "surprise contender," according to Mariani. "The year before, only a couple guys got any varsity time, so we were an unknown quantity for sure. Our team ended up being the right mix of a tough defensive team and high scoring offense."

Holy Cross had "strength down low

130

in Tom McDermott and Scott Mandy. Chris Hamel had an incredible knack for the ball and had to lead the league in steals that year," continues Mariani. "Bob Lasbury brought leadership and defense to the table and our backcourt, led by Rob Paternostro and myself, was pretty tough, too."

Mariani served as the Crusaders' top shooter while Paternostro earned All-City and All-NVL honors as top point guard in the league.

"Rob's ability to find the open man, to score and make big plays in big moments was a huge differentiator for us," says Mariani. "For us, it really came down to great team chemistry where everyone knew their role and played it well."

Holy Cross kept pace with Kennedy until the final week in 1989-90, before falling in overtime to the Eagles on a Mike Byrd three-pointer at the buzzer. The dramatic finish gave Jack Taglia's Kennedy squad a second consecutive NVL crown.

Ryan Sullivan

"What no one remembers before Byrd's shot is that in Kennedy's scramble coming out of a timeout, Malik Williams and Jerome Malloy both grabbed the ball at the same time after the ref placed it on the ground. It could have been ruled a turnover, but no call was made."

While Holy Cross may have been the surprise in 1989-90, Wilby played that role the next season, as Reggie O'Brien fielded a young Wildcat team that preferred a running and pressing style of play.

"Kennedy was again the NVL favorite in 1990-91, and listed by some polls as number one in Connecticut, while we were considered last among city teams and

not on the radar in any state polls," recalls Manny Wright of Wilby. "But we beat Kennedy in the first game of the season. Although we were young, we were talented and had a confidence about us."

Wright considers that season, his junior year, as "perhaps the most competitive and balanced year in league history. Every city team could have and legitimately had a shot to win the league."

As Crosby's Sullivan notes, there was a mathematical chance for an eventual five-way tie for first place with two rounds of games left to play that year. In the end, Kennedy and Wilby finished level at the top of the standings, requiring a one-game playoff to determine the champion.

The extra game went down to the wire, with Kennedy outlasting Wilby, 93-89, to earn a third straight NVL crown. Malik Williams, who combined with Jerome Malloy to score 69 points that night, hit two free throws with 28 seconds remaining to break an 89-89 tie with 28 seconds remaining in the game.

"Ultra-competitive" is the word used by Williams when looking back on that season. "There were no easy city games."

Williams and Malloy of Kennedy would be named to identical All-City and All-NVL teams, which also included fellow seniors Rob Paternostro of Holy Cross, Harun Ramey of Crosby and Sacred Heart's Brendan McCarthy.

"I realize that many great players and teams have come through both the city and NVL both before and after the 1990-91 season," says Crosby's Sullivan. "But overall, looking at each city team and the players they had, that was the best. Each game felt like a championship."

1991-92: Wright, Robinson lead Wilby to NVL title, CIAC semifinal

One year after the Naugatuck Valley League featured its most competitive race for a conference title, the 1991-92 season seemed a runaway by comparison – as Wilby won its first 13 league contests and cruised to its first NVL crown since 1985-86.

Reggie O'Brien's Wildcats returned the bulk of a team that had lost to Kennedy in a one-game playoff for the 1991 trophy, led by senior guard Manny Wright and juniors Marcus Robinson and Terrence Lott.

Each of the other city schools had to fill multiple starting positions left open by graduation, with the likes of Jerome Malloy, Harun Ramey, Rob Paternostro and Brendan McCarthy moving on to college.

Torrington – featuring the inside-outside duo of Brian Anzellotti and Dave Dmowski – and Naugatuck were expected to challenge some city squads and settle into spots in the upper half of the standings.

But the favored Wilby side made it known early which team would be in command at the very top.

Before its league campaign began, Wilby opened the season by playing two games in the Manchester Rotary Club Classic. Defending state champion Warren Harding of Bridgeport defeated the Wildcats in the opener, 84-72, but Wilby rebounded to beat host Manchester 72-68 in the consolation game.

Manny Wright

Manny Wright scored 15 of his team's 18 fourth-quarter points in that victory, the first game of a long winning streak for Reggie O'Brien's squad.

Employing a pressure defense and high-paced offense, Wilby raced through the first half of its NVL schedule, with Wright and Marcus Robinson assuming most of the scoring load.

While Wilby was cruising, a few other teams were battling it out for second place in the league. Torrington and Crosby showed promise early with each winning seven of their first ten league contests.

Two of Crosby's three losses were overtime defeats at the hands of Wilby. The Bulldogs held a six-point lead in the fourth-quarter of the second contest. But some poor foul shooting and a couple of turnovers turned the game in Wilby's favor. Terrence Lott led the Wildcats with 21 points in the 62-59 win, while Harvey Potts scored 15 for Crosby.

Defending champion Kennedy endured a three-game losing skein early, before the Eagles began moving up the standings. The skid ended when Trevor Morris beat the buzzer to knock off Holy Cross, 63-61, at the Crusaders' gym. Garnett Petteway led Kennedy with 21 points – including the 1,000 point of his career – while Brian Davis of Holy Cross had a game-high 30 points.

Back at the top, Wilby nearly hit the century mark in three straight games.

Robinson poured in 35 points in a 106-76 home win over Torrington; Wright hit for 29 and Terrence Lott recorded 22 points and 12 rebounds in a 99-32 rout of Watertown; and the team scored 38 first-quarter points en route to a 104-71 defeat of Sacred Heart.

The Wildcats' win streak – which had reached 13 games – then came to an end with a visit to the Pit at Holy Cross. Wilby had a double-digit lead in the second half, before Brian Davis took over the game for the Crusaders, scoring 25 of his team's 29 points in the final period to spark the upset.

Davis' basket with two minutes left in the game gave Holy Cross its first lead since the game's opening minutes. The junior guard, who finished with 36 points on the night, then converted four foul shots in the final minute to secure the 64-61 home win for the Crusaders.

Gaining confidence from the victory, Holy Cross went on to defeat Crosby, 61-50, in its next outing. Chris McGuire netted 16 points for the victorious Crusaders, while Chris Ortiz, Shawn McCarvell and John Gatling all hit double figures for the Bulldogs.

Holy Cross would claim victory in its final eight games of the regular season to finish 13-5 in the NVL – tied for second place with Kennedy – and head into state tournament play with plenty of momentum.

Wilby remained comfortable at the top and recovered with a pair of wins to clinch the league title. Naugatuck was able to slow the pace a bit against the Wildcats, but Wilby claimed a 76-72 road victory to ensure a share of the league crown. And the title was officially in Wilby's hands after cruising past Kennedy, with Wright and Robinson combining for 55 points.

Wright, the 5-11 senior, then scored

Contributed by Holy Cross High School

Brian Davis of Holy Cross helped lead the Crusaders to the semifinals of the CIAC Class LL tournament and was named to the 1991-92 All-City and All-NVL teams.

36 points, including the 1,000th point of his scholastic career, as Wilby trounced Wolcott 110-77 in its final game of the regular season.

Ranked third in the state in the New Haven Register's Top Ten poll, Wilby was seeded fifth in the Class L division of the CIAC tournament. Kennedy and Kaynor Tech were other Waterbury teams qualifying in Class L, while Holy Cross and Crosby represented the city in the Class LL bracket.

After compiling a 13-7 record that included a win over Naugatuck, Kaynor's postseason experience lasted just one game. Middletown built a 12-point halftime lead and held on for a 6-45 home win. Jason Arnauckas finished off a fine career at Kaynor by netting a game-high 22 points for the Panthers.

Kennedy fared better in its L open-

The 1991-92 Wilby Wildcats gather for a team photo at the school.

er, with reserve Andre Paris' 19 points leading five Eagles in double figures in a 84-71 home win over Killingly. But the CIAC bracket then paired the Eagles against city foe Wilby, which had overwhelmed Hand of Madison, 96-47, in the first round.

The third game of the season between Waterbury rivals was much closer than the first two. Looking to pull the upset, Kennedy held a five-point lead midway through the fourth period. But Wilby relied on its defensive pressure to spark a dramatic rally in the final four minutes to keep its season alive.

The Wildcats' 97-91 win included one of the best performances of the season from center Eddie Hicks, who registered 16 points and 14 rebounds. Manny Wright and Marcus Robinson topped 20 points in Wilby's 20th win of the season. Dennis Iverson collected 25 points and six assists while both Garnett and Garrett Petteway scored 19 for Kennedy, whose season ended with a 15-7 record.

In the Class L quarterfinals, Wilby outscored Guilford 33-20 in the third period to break open a tight game. The 88-67 victory over the fourth seed earned the Wildcats a second consecutive appearance in a CIAC semifinal.

Aiming for its first berth in a state final in nine years, Wilby was doomed by a poor shooting performance against East Catholic of Manchester. Down by double digits by halftime, the Wildcats couldn't muster enough of a second-half rally and were eliminated by a 91-75 scoreline. Marcus Robinson netted 35 points in the loss for Reggie O'Brien's Wildcats, who ended the season at 21-3. Manny Wright, who scored 11 in the semifinal loss, was named to the New Haven Register's All-State team.

The Class LL tournament saw another Waterbury school reach the semifinal round, as Holy Cross built on its late-season winning streak to produce a deep postseason run.

The 14th-seeded Crusaders faced a familiar foe in its LL opener, using a second-quarter run to open up a double-digit lead over Naugatuck. Chris McGuire led Holy Cross with 18 points while Derreck Gray added 13 in the 50-40 defeat of the Greyhounds.

Free-throw shooting proved crucial for Holy Cross in a second-round upset win over third-seeded Simsbury. Clinging to a slim lead in the final period, the Crusader trio of Brian Davis, Dave DiGiovanna and Chris McGuire combined to hit eight of ten foul shots in the last three minutes to secure a 53-52 victory and extend the team's winning streak to ten games.

The run for Ed Generali's Crusaders continued against another higher-ranked team in the quarterfinals. Trailing sixth-seeded Westhill of Stamford by 13 points in the third period, Holy Cross staged a late rally to send the game to overtime.

Brian Davis, injured earlier in the game, hit two three-pointers in the opening minute of the fourth period to fuel the comeback. The junior guard's bucket midway through the period gave the Crusaders the lead, but the 32 minutes of regulation time could not determine a winner.

Chris McGuire scored six of the Cru-saders' 12 points in the extra session, and the Waterbury team claimed a 69-64 victory to move on to the semifinals. After starting the season with a 6-6 record, Holy Cross was one win away from playing for a state title.

But facing a much bigger Stamford team and with Brian Davis hobbling due to a knee injury sustained against Westhill, the Crusaders were eliminated in the semifinals. Stamford used an 18-2 surge to take a 19-point lead at the half. Holy Cross endured a tough shooting night and couldn't recover, falling by a 81-43 scoreline. Tyrone Powell's 19 points led second-seeded Stamford while Davis and Chris McGuire scored 10 points each in the Crusaders' finale.

Davis would join the Wilby pair of Manny Wright and Marcus Robinson and Garnett Petteway of Kennedy on the All-City and All-NVL teams for the 1991-92 season. Crosby's Shawn McCarvell was also selected to the first-team All-City squad, while Torrington's Brian Anzellotti was the fifth member of the All-NVL team.

Kennedy's Petteway received the Billy Finn Award as the top senior in the city, and the Lt. Jack Cullinan Award for sportsmanship went to Wilby's Wright.

Wright's circuitous journey to achieve his PhD retains hometown focus

Ask most high school hoopsters from Waterbury where they hope their athletic talents will take them, and you'll hear that many dream of a future playing at a major college arena, such as UConn's Gampel Pavilion, Cameron Indoor Stadium at Duke or maybe one of the famous venues in the Big Ten conference.

A number from the city have been lucky enough to reach that level and hear their name called at one of the biggest stages in college basketball, given the opportunity to build on their achievements at the scholastic level.

But when the name of James "Manny" Wright was announced at the Breslin Center – home to Tom Izzo's Michigan State University team — it wasn't for anything basketball-related. It was to receive his PhD in educational administration and leadership at the 2017 graduation ceremony held at that arena, from the school whose graduate studies in education are ranked tops in the nation in that discipline.

Wright – a 1992 graduate of Wilby High who was named to the New Haven Register's All-State team after helping to lead the Wildcats to an NVL championship that year – didn't pursue any basketball offers after high school. He headed south for a few semesters at Virginia State University before moving to Atlanta, unsure of a specific field to pursue at the time.

The advice of Chris Love, another city hoopster who had pursued his PhD – before being shot and killed while a doctoral student at the University of Rhode Island in 1993 – remained with Wright during that period of uncertainty.

Love, an All-City performer at Kennedy High before earning a degree from Fairfield University, "saw the potential in me, and was afraid I would waste it," says Wright, who like many in Waterbury was devastated by the news of Love's tragic passing. "Remembering his words from our talks kept me headed in the right direction on my journey."

That journey led to Cairo, Egypt, where Wright spent a number of years working as an administrator for international schools in the city. Into his 30s, his path gained focus and he re-committed to pursuing higher education toward an advanced degree.

In addition to a bachelor's degree from Post University, he has since earned an MBA from Southern Connecticut State University and the doctorate from Michigan State. Wright's achievements have taken him out West; he currently works as an assistant professor at San Diego State University.

He has three sons – ages 11, 14, and 16 – and "raising them and following their endeavors over the years have been the biggest highlight of my life," says Wright. "My hoops career ended after high school, aside from recreational games."

But the memories of those scholastic exploits remain for the former star guard, who was one of four members of the 1991-92 Wilby team to finish their high school careers as 1,000-point scorers. Marcus Robinson, Terrence Lott and DeVonne Parker also eventually reached that landmark after being contributors for that 1992 team, which went 19-1 in league play to end Kennedy's three-year run of NVL championships.

"That team was a close-knit group.

Many of us hung out together after school and on the weekends, and we even committed to running cross-country in the offseason to help prepare," remembers Wright. "We were fearless, athletic, and we embodied the persona of living and growing up in the roughest neighborhoods in the North End.

"Growing up in those environments is what gave us our edge, and coach Reg (O'Brien) cultivated and nurtured that edge and did not seek for us to change; instead he embraced us," adds Wright.

Wilby's 1992 NVL title, the second of three during O'Brien's tenure as coach, came one year after the Wildcats were defeated by Kennedy in a playoff for the 1990-91 league trophy (after the two schools compiled identical 17-3 regular-season records).

"That 90-91 year, my junior year, was perhaps the most competitive and balanced year in league history. Every city team could have and legitimately had a shot to win the league," recalls Wright.

"The thing about that season was that if you looked at the preseason impressions,

James 'Manny' Wright

Kennedy was the NVL favorite, and listed by some polls as number one in Connecticut, while we were picked last among city teams and not on the radar in any state polls" continued Wright. "We hosted Kennedy in the first game of the season, and even though they returned their best players in Jerome Malloy and Malik Williams, we just had a confidence about us and claimed victory. It may have been seen as a surprising result, but we were a young, talented team and put the city, the NVL and the whole state on notice with the win. It was one of the most memorable games for me as it kicked off a magical run over my final two years of

high school."

The 5-foot-11 inch Wright and backcourt mate Robinson emerged as one of the top guard combinations in the league that season, leading the Wildcats to a 17-3 record in the NVL before dropping the championship playoff. Wilby would finish with a 20-5 overall record, advancing all the way to the CIAC Class M semifinals before falling to perennial power and eventual Class M state champion Warren Harding of Bridgeport.

With most of the team back for the 1991-92 season – and other city schools having lost players to graduation – Wilby cruised through a 19-1 regular season to earn a top-five ranking in both the Hartford Courant and New Haven Register's Top 10 polls of Connecticut teams.

The Wilby-Kennedy rivalry extended into the CIAC tournament that season, with the city rivals meeting in a Class L second-round game. Wright's Wildcats had comfortably won the two regular-season contests, but found themselves down late in the fourth quarter of the state tourney game.

"Jerome Malloy and Malik Williams had graduated but Kennedy still had the Petteway brothers (Garnett and Garrett), and they were beating us all game," recalls Wright. "With a few minutes left in the game and a Kennedy player at the foul line, we had hung our heads, I think conceding defeat."

A Kennedy substitute took his place in the lane, "announcing to his teammates that they had practice the next day after school … implying that they had won and their season would continue and ours would end with the loss," says Wright.

"With that, we all lifted our heads and Marcus Robinson said, 'we'll see about that,'" says Wright.

Wilby then picked up its game and scored 10 points in a row for a comeback victory.

"In the closing seconds we were on the line shooting, and in between foul shots Marcus came in and announced, 'we have practice tomorrow at 2:00,'" adds Wright. "The late turnaround was easily one of the grittiest moments in my Wilby career. It personified who we were."

The Wildcats would again reach the CIAC semifinal round before falling, this time to East Catholic of Manchester. In addition to the All-State honor in his senior season, Wright was named to the All-City and All-NVL teams and was the recipient of the Lt. Jack Cullinan Award for sportsmanship among city seniors.

Playing during a period that featured so many talented players from the city, Wright mentions Malloy and Williams of Kennedy, Crosby's Harun Ramey and Rob Paternostro of Holy Cross as among the best from that time.

"All the city schools were strong, Sacred Heart also had a solid group of players that were formidable as a team," says Wright – who adds a name that never made it on to a city high school roster: "Rob Munn ("Squirt") was up at the head of the pack, when you talk about players from that period. I think it was known from when we were young that Squirt was the best. Malloy emerged as the best, but Squirt never got the chance to showcase in the NVL," says Wright.

Munn was in and out of schools and

"would have graduated in 1991 or 1992 and been among the best in the state," believes Wright. "To anyone that knew him, I imagine it would be hard to argue otherwise," says Wright.

"If you put Squirt on any of the city teams in 1991, they are the clear league and probably state favorite," believes Wright. "I lobbied hard to get him to come to Wilby, but life circumstances led him down a different path. Many of us, especially those of us in the public schools, were lured by the streets – and for those of us dedicated, focused, and good enough to play hoop, we had a viable alternative."

Munn's story reflects the challenges faced by students in urban school districts. These challenges are a focus of Wright's current work as assistant professor of educational leadership at San Diego State University. "My research agenda centers on social justice in education, specifically the ways that culturally responsive school practices can impact educational opportunities and outcomes for students from environments much like the North End neighborhoods where I was raised," says Wright.

His journey may have taken a circuitous route, but James "Manny" Wright has found his path in life – building on his experiences to broaden understanding of the organizational currents that affect schooling and help guide a pathway toward more effective community engagement within educational reform.

1992-93: Wildcats complete undefeated league season

A pair of early-season landmark achievements helped to kickstart the 1992-93 NVL basketball season, which would culminate with another bit of history when Wilby captured a second consecutive league crown and became the first undefeated NVL champion in more than a decade.

The Wildcats looked every bit the part of the favorite in their league opener, when senior Marcus Robinson surpassed 1,000 points for his career in a 96-74 romp over Crosby. The 6-1 Robinson ended the night with 26 points and all five Wilby starters scored in double figures.

Rob Saunders led Crosby with 21 points and Jose Malave added 14 for the Bulldogs, who would win two of their next three games to give Nick Augelli 200 victories as head coach at Crosby. Four Bulldog players hit double figures in win number 200, a 76-54 triumph at Watertown.

A Torrington defeat of Holy Cross allowed Wilby to take over sole possession of first place in the NVL standings on January 8, a night when the Wildcats' up-tempo transition game fueled a 105-75 rout of Sacred Heart. Damien Manning scored 18 points and DeVonne Parker added 17 to complement Marcus Robinson's scoring as Wilby moved to 5-0 in league games.

Parker, an imposing sophomore forward, then collected 28 points and 20 rebounds in a 79-70 Wilby win at Naugatuck – as coach Reggie O'Brien's Wildcats began to pull away from the field at the top of the standings.

Kennedy used a deliberate game plan to slow Wilby a bit in its next outing, and even held a 10-point lead over the Wildcats in the third period. But a 22-6 scoring run sparked Wilby to a 59-49 home win. Robinson and Parker combined for 34 points for Wilby, while Garrett Petteway tallied a game-high 24 points as Kennedy dropped to 4-3 in the league (and 6-3 overall).

The Eagles rebounded from the loss by outlasting Crosby, 63-56, at the Palace. Petteway was high scorer with 25 points for Kennedy, which gained control late in a game that was tied after three periods. Terrance Morrison and Armand LeVasseur also hit double digits for the Eagles, while Mike Weaver and Jose Malave combined for 32 points for an undermanned Crosby team that had to deal with injuries for most of the campaign.

Across town that night, Holy Cross senior Brian "T" Davis scored 33 points for Holy Cross as the Crusaders defeated Sacred Heart, 79-69, to solidify a hold on second place. Derek Gray and Harold Miller also reached double figures for Holy Cross, offsetting a 32-point night from Mike Sanders of Sacred Heart.

Torrington and Kennedy would represent the main challengers to Holy Cross for second place in the NVL as the season progressed. Showing much improvement from a couple of seasons earlier – when suburban teams went 0-50 in league games against city schools in 1990-91 – Torrington, Naugatuck and Ansonia all produced solid seasons and claimed a number of victories against teams from Waterbury.

Ansonia nearly pulled off the upset of the season against Wilby, but was defeated 95-93 in overtime by the visiting Wildcats in a mid-season contest. Marcus Robinson's jumper with 24 seconds left in the extra session provided the winning points. Rob Sanders of Ansonia scored 37 points in the loss, matching Robinson's total as high scorers on the night.

Torrington won seven straight games at one point, culminating with a 44-43 win at Kennedy when big man Dave Dmowski hit a free throw with one second left on the clock. Ralph Calabrese netted 13 points while Garrett Petteway and Marcus Taylor each hit double figures for the Eagles.

Wilby would end the Torrington streak, winning 77-63 on the Raiders' court. Devonne Parker scored 22 points for the visiting Wildcats, who raced to a 23-7 first-quarter lead and coasted to victory.

Reggie O'Brien's Wildcats then captured their ninth straight game by outgunning Crosby 121-106 on January 29th – ending the month as the fifth-ranked team in Connecticut in the weekly coaches poll. Four Wildcat players scored more than 20 points in the high-scoring affair, led by Terrance Lott's 27 points. Marcus Robinson (20), Damien Manning (23) and DeVonne Parker (21) also topped that mark for Wilby, which led 59-44 at halftime.

"If someone told me we would score 106 points and lose, I'd tell them they were crazy," said Crosby coach Nick Augelli to the *Waterbury Republican*. Bulldog forward Chris Ortiz netted a career-high 45 points as the team dropped to 3-6 in the league.

That same night, Kennedy avenged an earlier loss to Holy Cross by throttling the Crusaders 70-42. Garrett Pettteway hit 17 of 25 shots to record a career-high 39 points, while Terrance Morrison excelled on the defensive end by holding Crusader star Brian Davis to 20 points as the Eagles improved to 6-4 in the league.

Sacred Heart evened its NVL record at 5-5 with a thrilling 84-82 win at Naugatuck. Greg Sullivan drove the length of the floor to lay in the winning hoop with five seconds remaining for the Hearts, who scored the last nine points of the game to complete a dramatic comeback. Sullivan would duplicate the feat later in the season, taking the ball the full length

Contributed / Wilby High School

The 1992-93 Naugatuck Valley League champion Wilby Wildcats

to hit a basket just before the overtime buzzer sounded to defeat Crosby, 71-70.

The Hearts put together a fine second half of the season and would finish 12-6 in the league, tied with Catholic school rival Holy Cross for third place.

Holy Cross finally got the chance to face Wilby in mid-February, due to earlier postponements. The Wildcats held a slim, two-point lead at the half but ramped up its defensive pressure after the break to pull away for a 96-81 victory as it moved closer to a second consecutive NVL crown. Four players hit double figures for Wilby while Derek Gray and Harold Miller combined for 40 points for Holy Cross in the loss.

The Crusaders rebounded to top Torrington, with senior Brian Davis becoming the seventh player in school history to score more than 1,000 career points.

The 1,000-point plateau was reached by another performer a week later, when Wilby senior Terrence Lott hit for 12 points in a 89-80 victory over Naugatuck. Lott's classmate Marcus Robinson led the way with 24 points in the home win, which clinched a share of the league title for Wilby.

With games against city foes Kennedy and Holy Cross left on its schedule, Wilby's quest wasn't fully complete. But the Wildcats used its full-court press early against Kennedy to build a 30-12 lead. Jack Taglia's Eagles fought back to within a point, but Wilby made some key plays down the stretch to secure an 87-84 victory. Lott had 21 points and Robinson scored 20 for Wilby; Garrett Petteway netted a game-high 34 points while 6-9 Marcus Taylor added 17 for Kennedy, which would finish in second place in the league standings

With the title in hand, Wilby then completed its next goal of an undefeated NVL season by defeating Wolcott at home and then downing Holy Cross on the road.

The Wolcott win came easy – with the Wildcats scoring a school-record 141 points and senior Marcus Robinson breaking Phil Lott's school record by pouring in 61 points on the night. The senior guard's total included 11 three-pointers – believed to be a state record at the time – and came on the same day of the year (February 13) that Crosby's Harun Ramey had set the city record with 68 points in 1990.

Terrence Lott

Robinson settled for half that amount (30 points) in Wilby's regular-season finale at Holy Cross, a 95-75 triumph that secured a perfect 18-0 record in NVL contests. Brian Davis, who scored 37 points, kept the Crusaders in the game early before the visiting Wildcats claimed control by halftime. Terrence Lott and DeVonne Parker combined for 48 points for Wilby, which had not lost a game since its season opener against Warren Harding of Bridgeport.

At 19-1 overall, Wilby was selected as top seed in the Class L tournament, one of three city schools qualifying for that division. The others included Kennedy and Kaynor Tech – the city's technical school that had put together a fine season in the Vo-Tech League behind the play of Steve Tsaprazis, Miguel Bao and George Monteiro.

Kaynor Tech used an 11-0 run in the second quarter to oust Wilcox Tech of Meriden, 69-65, in its opener, to advance to the second round of the CIAC tournament for the first time in five years. Third-seeded Guilford then knocked out the 14th-seeded Panthers, 85-68, at that stage, with Bao and Monteiro combining for 53 points for Kaynor in the loss.

Top-seeded Wilby, which received a first-round bye, faced an NVL foe in its first postseason game. Marcus Robinson canned six three-pointers and scored 32 points as the Wildcats routed Torrington, 99-53. DeVonne Parker added 16 and Terrance Lott had 15 in Wilby's 20th victory of the season.

Another familiar foe represented Wilby's opponent in the L quarterfinals. Kennedy had knocked off Seymour – 60-50, behind big man Marcus Taylor's 16 points – to reach that stage and earn a postseason game against Wilby for a second straight season.

Proving the adage that it's tough to beat a team three times in a season, Kennedy staged a dramatic comeback and sent the quarterfinal to overtime when Garrett Petteway's three-pointer fell through the net before the final buzzer.

And the underdog Eagles went on to pull out an 82-81 overtime victory, with Terrance Morrison's driving bucket providing the winning margin with 20 seconds left in the extra session. Petteway finished with 33 points, while Morrison, Steve Fillie and Bobby Nealy also hit double figures for Kennedy. Terrence Lott scored 26 while Marcus Robinson and DeVonne Parker added 16 each for Wilby, which ended its season at 20-2.

Kennedy advanced to play defending state champion St. Joseph of Trumbull in the semifinals. The fifth-seeded Cadets built on a six-point halftime lead with a

Mike Sanders

strong third quarter and pulled away for a 62-41 win.

Maurice Howell scored 19, Desmond Artis had 12 and 6-9 center Keith Vail played well down the stretch for St. Joseph, who would go on to repeat as Class L champions. Marcus Taylor – Kennedy's own 6-9 big man – outscored Vail 10 to 8 for the night and Garrett Petteway contributed 12 points for Kennedy, which ended the season with a 17-6 record.

Sacred Heart qualified for the Class M tournament and impressed in its opener, as Mike Sanders' 32 points led the team past Immaculate of Danbury, 63-50. The Hearts were then tied at halftime with Trinity Catholic in their next game, before falling to the second-seeded team by a 79-57 scoreline. Sanders and Shawn Bazemore combined for 35 points for 13-9 Sacred Heart.

Holy Cross matched the Heart's two-game postseason run upon qualifying in the Class LL bracket. The Crusaders topped Hillhouse, 94-88, in a first-round game – with senior Brian Davis pouring in a career-high 43 points – before running into Hartford Public, the top-ranked team in the state that featured 6-11 All-American Marcus Camby.

The UMass-bound Camby, who missed much of the first half due to foul trouble, returned to contribute 14 points and nine blocks as the Hartford school pulled away for a 97-62 second-round win over the Crusaders. Keith Kendall led the 24-0 Owls with 19 points, while Davis and Derek Gray combined for 30 points for Holy Cross, which finished 13-9 on the season.

Augelli looks back on storied career

Interviewed for a game report after registering the 200th victory of his coaching career on January 8, 1993, Crosby High coach Nick Augelli told Waterbury Republican reporter Tim Yagle that he never thought he would be coaching long enough to achieve that number of wins.

"It wasn't even a goal of mine when I started coaching. When I was assistant coach for 10 years, and then became the varsity coach (in 1979), I didn't think I'd last another 13 years," said Augelli. "It's a long time to coach, especially after you've been an assistant. I thought I would be burned out."

Amazingly, nearly thirty years after making that statement, Augelli is still on the Crosby bench and piling up victories, with no burnout in sight. The man who didn't think he would reach 200 victories has now surpassed 700 wins, and is the second all-time winningest coach in Connecticut high school basketball history (behind Vito Montelli of St. Joseph of Trumbull).

He doubled the 200 victories in March of 2005, getting career win number 400 when the Bulldogs defeated Fitch of Groton in a CIAC tournament game – on their way to an undefeated season and a state title (the second of three CIAC crowns for Augelli as coach). That 2005 Crosby team, featuring Julian Allen, James "Bootsy" Moore and Damien Saunders, is considered one of the best squads ever in city annals.

Augelli hasn't quite yet doubled the 400 victories, but captured his 700th win in February 2020 when the Bulldogs downed Waterbury Career Academy.

"When I reached my 100th, that was special. It meant a lot," stated Augelli in 1993. "When you're in coaching for so long, there's only so much that's going to

make an impact on you. This is nice because I stuck it out. And I didn't expect it."

What kept Augelli around for win 200 still applies today. "A fondness for the game and for the players," he says, has kept him on the bench.

"To this day I still see many of my former players and I feel so proud when I see them do well, both professionally and in basketball, in their career choices," says Augelli. "To me, the greatest part of coaching is seeing the players progress in becoming individuals with great character and people that I can be proud to say that I coached."

Having a couple of long-time assistants by his side has also played a role in Augelli's longevity. "I have been blessed by having two coaches – Larry DeVito as junior varsity coach and volunteer assistant Billy Mahoney – who have been with me for over 26 years each," add Augelli.

"Without them I would not have had the success I have had over the years. It has made things a little easier for me because they are able to do a lot of the things I do not have time to do, and that makes coaching that much more enjoyable for me."

Augelli began as a volunteer assistant at Crosby, even before the school had moved into the Pierpont Road site it has called home for some 47 years now. The year was 1969, when he began coaching the Bulldogs' freshman team in his second year of teaching at the high school, then located in downtown Waterbury.

One year later, he was junior varsity coach and assistant to head coach Bob Brown, "who has been both a mentor and a friend since that time," notes Augelli. "We still get together regularly to have coffee."

Crosby coach Nick Augelli pictured in 2021 with two of his former players who were named Billy Finn Award winners for their senior seasons with the Bulldogs: Willie Davis, left, winner in 1985-86, and cousin Justin Davis, the 2019-2020 recipient.

Augelli learned the structure of the game and how to conduct a practice from Brown. "Some of the things Bobby did when he coached we still use today," says Augelli. "A lot of the drills for defense and offense have been adapted to today's game with the implementation of the three-point shot, but the basics are still the same.

"Bobby's style and my style were completely different and that's why we complemented each other; so, I can honestly say that the things that I learned from Bobby is what made me a successful basketball coach," adds Augelli.

The 1974-75 season was a landmark

for the Crosby basketball program. That school year, Crosby relocated from its downtown location to an expansive complex on Pierpont Road that housed the high school and adjoining Wallace Middle School, along with a state-of-the-art gymnasium that was dubbed "The Crosby Palace."

"When it opened, it was quite a gym with movable, portable baskets and probably one of the largest seating-capacity gyms in the state," says Augelli. "For years we had to practice at Kennedy and were fit in between Kennedy's team and Mattatuck Community College. So, having the new school and gym open up was a great advantage for us. We could practice more and truly have a home court."

Its original bleachers have since been replaced, with a reduced capacity, but the original setup was built to hold 2,800 sitting fans.

The Bulldogs' initial season in their new home was one to remember. Led by star guard Steve Johnson and fellow junior Pete Anton, Crosby played an entertaining style, running and pressing its way to a 12-2 league record and a first Naugatuck Valley League title under Brown – who still keeps in regular contact with Augelli.

Crosby made deep runs in the Class L tournament both that season and the next, only to fall to state power Warren Harding of Bridgeport both years.

Brown would coach the Bulldogs to

one more NVL title before handing the reins over to Augelli for the 1979-80 campaign, when Crosby again fell just one game short of a CIAC final appearance.

The elusive state title would come in 1998, the first of Crosby's three CIAC championships during the Augelli era. Dhaamin Hill and Marvin Rountree were top 'Dogs that season, which culminated in a victory over Notre Dame of West Haven in the Class L championship game.

Augelli would guide Crosby teams to five CIAC final appearances over the 12 seasons between 1998 and 2009, winning again in 2005 and 2008.

With the three CIAC titles and more than 700 wins, the court and gymnasium at Crosby are now named in his honor.

"The 2015 dedication of Coach Nick Augelli Court and the naming of the gym in my honor in 2019 is something that I really cherish," says Augelli, who has been on the sidelines since the gym's opening in 1974.

Appearing in six CIAC state championship games have provided plenty of memories for Augelli. When asked if there's one game at the Crosby gym that might stand out among the rest, Augelli recalls the 1987 Crosby-Wilby matchup that determined the NVL champion that season. Both teams were 18-1 at the time and both ranked in the Top 10 poll of state teams.

"A portion of the bleachers had broken and the Park Department had to bring in extra bleachers. But they just let everybody into the gym. There were over 3,000 people, with many standing on the sidelines and under the basket," recalls Augelli. "As the game turned out, we were down by 22 at halftime and then scored 60 points in the second half to win by one point in overtime."

Besides all the games that were played over the years at the gym, "the practices and the times spent with the many players and seeing those players achieve their goals is what stands out the most for me," adds Augelli.

"As I said before, I have been lucky to have had such great players and individuals that made coaching enjoyable and very rewarding for me," continues Augelli. "I still have the drive in me to create a team and to mold individuals into a winning team year in and year out. When I do not have that drive or when I take it as a job, then I know it will be time to retire."

For the man who initially didn't think he'd be around too many years as head coach, the time spent with his players at the 47-year-old gym that now bears his name continues to grow.

"Someday I would like to calculate the number of hours I have spent in that gymnasium – between practices, games and preparation for each season. It would be quite a number," says Augelli.

1993-94: Crusaders outlast Crosby, Ansonia to capture NVL title

Any doubts that the 1993-94 NVL basketball season would be more competitive than the previous year — when Wilby cruised through an undefeated league season — were answered after the Wildcats' league opener, when Ansonia rallied for 64-63 home win over the defending champions. The Chargers' comeback included eight straight points in the final two minutes, with two free throws from Rob Sanders giving the hosts the lead with 24 seconds remaining. But the victory wasn't sealed until Wilby's Rodney Cunningham missed a three-pointer in the closing seconds.

Sanders and Chris Zuraw combined for 46 points on the night for Ansonia, a team that featured size and athleticism and would position itself among the contenders challenging for the league title. The frontline for Coach Ed Strumello's Chargers included 6-5 Steve Coughlin and 6-7 Len Svelnys to battle such opposing big men as Wilby's 6-8 center Tavares Anderson, 6-7 Ryan Brown of Watertown, Crosby's 6-7 center Charron Watson and 6-5 Bill Cain of Naugatuck.

The NVL's list of big men for 1993-94 also included 6-8 freshman Edmund Saunders – the most prized newcomer in the state, who opted to enroll at Holy Cross. Coach Ed Generali's Crusaders had lost the talented Brian Davis to graduation, but returned an experienced backcourt led by Harold Miller and Derek Gray to complement Saunders and Paul Nardozzi in the paint.

Edmund Saunders' older brother Rob was one of the senior leaders at Crosby, along with Watson and Andre Johnson.

The Bulldogs were looking to rebound from a subpar 1992-93 campaign, and got their season off on a positive note by defeating Kennedy in their league opener.

The win was sparked by Crosby's defensive pressure, which enabled the hosts to build an early lead and hold on for a 75-54 win. Saunders and Watson combined for 32 points on the night and freshman Jayson Johnson added 10 points for the victors, while Armand LeVasseur and Steve Fillie led a young Kennedy team with 14 points apiece.

The Eagles rebounded nicely by holding off Ansonia, 47-46, when the Chargers' Steve Coughlin hit just one of two free throws with one second remaining that could have tied the game. Kennedy sophomore Marlin Parker, who would emerge as one of the league's surprise performers in 1993-94, netted 16 points in the win.

In another game that was decided on last-second foul shots, Holy Cross freshman Edmund Saunders hit a free throw with one second left to give the Crusaders a 64-63 come-from-behind win over Sacred Heart. The Hearts' 6-1 guard Mike Sanders had put on a show with 23 first-half points before Holy Cross rallied behind Harold Miller and Paul Nardozzi to improve to 4-0 on the season.

Wilby responded to its opening loss by winning two non-league contests and then routing a solid Torrington team to regain its footing. Senior Damien Manning collected 21 points and 9 assists and junior forward DeVonne Parker added 20 points and 15 rebounds in the 95-63 home win over the Raiders.

The 6-2 Parker produced two more double-double performances in Wildcat wins over Crosby and Naugatuck, to set up a clash with an undefeated Holy Cross team that was listed among the state's top ten teams by the *New Haven Register*.

The host Crusaders maintained a lead in the game until late in the third period, when Wilby went on a 14-0 run to secure the advantage and hold on for an 87-82 victory. Manning and Parker combined for 47 points in the Wildcats' road win, while Harold Miller hit for 26 points and Derek Gray had 21 in Holy Cross' first loss of the season.

The result left three teams – Ansonia, Holy Cross and Wilby – tied for first place in the NVL standings. And with two games separating six teams in the standings, a sense of parity had emerged in the NVL after Wilby's dominance the previous two seasons.

The competitiveness extended toward the bottom half of the standings, as evidenced by a pair of midseason games at Watertown. Led by Ryan Brown's 20 points and 21 rebounds, the Indians defeated Sacred Heart – in a game that saw the Hearts' Mike Sanders surpass the 1,000-point plateau for his career. Watertown then provided the upset of the season by knocking off Wilby, 90-87.

Crosby would put an end to Watertown's run, with Rob Saunders, Charron Watson and Jayson Johnson all reaching double figures in a 65-60 decision that was one of five straight wins for the Bulldogs.

The streak put Crosby in the thick of the NVL title race, moving ahead of Wilby in the standings. But the Bulldogs ran into a Holy Cross team that had piled up eight straight wins of its own. The Crusaders' produced a 89-71 home win – which featured its bench outscoring the Bulldog

Reprinted with permission of the Republican-American

Members of the *Waterbury Republican*'s 1993-94 All-NVL first team included Harold Miller of Holy Cross and Sacred Heart's Mike Sanders (front row), and Damien Manning of Wilby, Watertown's Ryan Brown and Rob Sanders of Ansonia (in back).

reserves by a 23-0 margin – to maintain a hold on the top spot with a few league games remaining.

Ansonia – sitting a game and a half behind Holy Cross – still had a say in the final standings, having to face the Crusaders and Crosby among its final three league contests. Aiming to seize the opportunity, the Chargers staged a late rally to edge Holy Cross, 61-58, and tighten the race. Robert Sanders hit for 21 points and Tim Lynch added 13 for Ansonia, who scored eight straight points midway through the fourth quarter on the way to a crucial home win.

The Chargers then dispatched Sacred Heart – with Chris Zuraw and Steve Coughlin the top scorers — before hosting Crosby in their final regular-season game. Ansonia again rallied late against a city opponent, tying the game at 64

Contributed by Holy Cross High School

Holy Cross guard Harold Miller puts up a shot in a game against Crosby. Miller and the Crusaders ended Wilby's two-year run of NVL titles by claiming the league crown in 1993-94.

after falling behind by double digits. But the visiting Bulldogs scored the final four points of the contest on foul shots — two each by senior Rob Saunders, who finished with 30 points, and freshman Jayson Johnson – to hold off the Chargers.

Both teams needed a Holy Cross loss the following night to be included in a three-way tie for first place, but the Crusaders downed Kennedy to claim their first NVL title under coach Ed Generali. Paul Nardozzi hit for 22 points and freshman big man Edmund Saunders scored 15 of his 19 in the first half as Holy Cross took control early and held on for the 84-71 win over the Eagles, who were led by Armand LeVasseur's five three-pointers and 21 points.

With winter weather having caused a number of cancellations during January and February, the NVL postponed a league tournament it had proposed to reinstate for the 1993-94 season. But the NVL's competitive regular season had certainly prepared the four city teams that qualified for the CIAC tournament.

Holy Cross, the highest rated team among the four, opened with an impressive win in the Class LL's first round. Edmund Saunders, the 6-8 freshman, produced his best performance of the season by notching 25 points, 16 rebounds and six blocked shot as the fifth-seeded Crusaders cruised past West Haven, 86-67. Guard Harold Miller matched Saunders' 25 points and senior Derek Gray added nine points and eight assists in the Crusaders' 18th victory of the season.

Holy Cross then faced a talented Windsor team that featured Keyon Smith and Russell Scott in the second round. The dramatic contest featured eight ties and eight lead changes before visiting Windsor escaped with a 77-75 decision. Senior Derek Gray scored 19 points in his final high school game while Harold Miller netted 15 for the Crusaders.

Crosby, seeded 15th in Class LL, also started with a commanding win. Big men Rob Saunders and Charron Watson combined for 50 points as the host Bulldogs coasted past Ridgefield, 75-54. The win earned Nick Augelli's team a game at second-seeded Warren Harding of Bridgeport, where Crosby's season ended with a 73-51 loss.

A pair of Waterbury teams fared better in the Class L bracket, as both Wilby and Kennedy advanced to the quarterfinals before falling.

Reggie O'Brien's Wildcats started slow in their opener against Farmington, before putting together a strong second half for a 90-78 victory. Junior DeVonne Parker collected 38 points and 14 rebounds in the home win.

Eighth-seeded Wilby continued its postseason by outlasting Bullard-Havens of Bridgeport, 76-63. Parker and senior Damien Manning combined for 49 points to offset Demetrius Dailey's 31 points as Wilby claimed its 16th win of the season.

Wilby's postseason run ended with an 80-75 loss to undefeated and top-seeded E.O. Smith in the quarterfinals. Manning was top scorer for the Wildcats with 25 points, while Rod Cunningham added 14 in a losing cause. E.O. Smith continued its unbeaten run by topping NVL member Ansonia in the semifinals.

Kennedy, which qualified for the CIAC tournament with a losing record of 8-12, was down by double digits in its first game at Bristol Central before rallying for a double-overtime victory. Marlin Park-er, who blocked a shot at the end of the first extra session, scored 26 points and Armand LeVasseur had 19 as the Eagles moved on via a 70-64 decision.

The 27th-seeded Eagles produced another surprising win in the second round in coasting past 11th-rated Newtown, 76-49. Kennedy's defense forced 27 turnovers in thwarting the higher seed's offense, while Parker and LeVasseur combined for 47 points in Kennedy's 10th win of the season.

Jack Taglia's Eagles nearly completed a hat trick of CIAC upsets, but fell to third-seeded St. Joseph of Trumbull in the L quarterfinals. Kennedy led 55-50 after three periods but then had three players foul out in the fourth quarter, and St. Joseph surged to a 76-64 victory.

Marlin Parker, who netted 23 points in Kennedy's quarterfinal loss, was named to the All-City second team for the 1993-94 season. The second team also included Harold Miller and Derek Gray of Holy Cross, Wilby's DeVonne Parker and Rodney Cunningham, Andre Johnson of Crosby and Sacred Heart's Shawn Bazemore.

The All-City first team featured Paul Nardozzi of Holy Cross, Wilby's Damien Manning, Mike Sanders of Sacred Heart and Crosby's Rob Saunders and Charron Watson.

Wilby's Manning and Sacred Heart's Sanders were also named to the All-NVL first team. They were joined by Harold Miller of Holy Cross, Robert Sanders of Ansonia and Ryan Brown of Watertown.

Sacred Heart's Sanders, who averaged 29 points a game for the season to lead the league, was named recipient of the year's Billy Finn Award. Crosby guard Andre Johnson was the winner of the Lt. Jack Cullinan Award, given each year to the senior who demonstrates the best sportsmanship.

1994-95: Holy Cross and Ansonia win CIAC state championships

The Naugatuck Valley League welcomed a number of new coaches – and a new school – for the 1994-95 basketball season, which would culminate in two league teams capturing state championships, the only time that has happened in the history of the conference.

Seymour High joined the league at the beginning of the school year, bringing the total number of NVL schools to 11. Four of the 11 would see different head coaches roaming their gyms' sidelines; and while that would seem quite a shakeup, two of the four were familiar faces within city and NVL hoop circles.

Joe Frascatore, replacing Chris Murphy at Sacred Heart, was an assistant to John Gilmore for the Hearts in the 1960s (and had coached Kennedy's Jack Taglia and Holy Cross' Ed Generali at the junior varsity level in those earlier days).

Down in Ansonia, Tom McQueeney returned as head coach, having previously helmed the Chargers basketball program from 1963 to 1988 (before serving as the school's girls basketball coach for five years).

Other new coaches included Kevin Wesche at Naugatuck – moving up from assistant after Joe DiStasio stepped down from the post – and John Minicucci at Wolcott, taking over a program in the midst of a 46-game losing streak.

While not part of the NVL, Kaynor Tech added to the area's coaching carousel for the 1994-95 season. Hank Spellman, who starred for the city's technical school during the mid-1970s, replaced Marty Sparano as the Panthers' head basketball coach after Sparano became the director of continuing education at the school.

Spellman at Kaynor and Frascatore at Sacred Heart would oversee rebuilding seasons at their respective schools, having lost some key players to graduation after the 1993-94 season. Marcus Stallworth and Craig Nelson would serve as leaders for Kaynor, while the Hearts would field a young team featuring junior guard Mike Sullivan and 6-4 Shawn Bazemore.

Sacred Heart claimed victory in one of two periods it played in the pre-season city jamboree, which was won by Kennedy after Jack Taglia's Eagles outlasted Wilby in the championship quarter. Kennedy returned a solid inside-outside combination in guard Armand LeVasseur and 6-4 forward Marlin Parker from a team that put together a surprising run to the CIAC quarterfinals after an 8-12 regular-season record in 1993-94.

Ansonia had gone even further than Kennedy in the previous year's postseason, and looked capable of repeating a deep run in CIAC play in McQueeney's return as coach. The Chargers featured a massive front line of 6-7 Len Svelnys, 6-7 Phil Mrazik and 6-5 Steve Coughlin, and featured four others 6-3 or taller in its pursuit of a first league title in 12 years.

While Ansonia's focus was its frontcourt, Crosby would rely on its guard play after losing big men Charron Watson and Rob Saunders to graduation. Sophomore Jayson Johnson and newcomer Chris Latham – a 5-11 transfer from Abbott Tech – were expected to shoulder the scoring load on a team that also included senior Tony Ortiz, a football All-Amer-

Contributed by Crosby High School

Edmund Saunders of Holy Cross battles Crosby's Tony Ortiz for a rebound during a Naugatuck Valley League game at Crosby. The Crusaders captured their second consecutive league title in 1994-95.

Crusaders, along with junior forwards Tom Platt and Mike Bolton.

Facing Catholic school rival Sacred Heart in its opening game, Holy Cross used a 12-0 second-quarter spurt to claim control. Harold Miller scored 27 points and Edmund Saunders contributed 16 points as the Crusaders cruised to a 75-58 victory.

The opening weekend of league play featured some intriguing matchups between title contenders. Ansonia visited Kennedy for a game that wasn't decided until the final buzzer, when Steve Coughlin's three-point attempt bounded off the rim to give the host Eagles a 69-68 win. The Kennedy defense was able to neutralize Ansonia's size, while Armand LeVasseur hit six three-pointers and scored 26 points for the victors. Coughlin and Len Svelnys combined for 30 points for Ansonia.

Wilby started with an impressive 89-72 home win over Crosby. DeVonne Parker poured in 36 points – including the 1,000th point of his career – for the Wildcats, who out-rebounded the smaller Bulldogs by a 42-18 margin.

Traveling north to Torrington for its first road game, Wilby started slowly and a late comeback fell short against the Raiders. Rick Koenig's shooting (31 points) keyed Torrington's 65-64 victory – the second year in a row it had defeated Wilby at the Connie Donahue gym – and showed that the experienced Raiders' squad was capable of going toe-to-toe with the league's top teams.

ican and track star who would go on to attend the University of Nebraska.

Wilby had its own imposing physical presence in DeVonne Parker. The 6-2 Parker was the top returning player for Reggie O'Brien's Wildcats, whose only loss in personnel from a 16-7 team was All-City and All-NVL performer Damien Manning.

Holy Cross had also lost an All-City first-teamer – in Paul Nardozzi – but went in to the season as league favorites. Senior guard Harold Miller and 6-8 sophomore Edmund Saunders – two of the top ten players in the state, according to the *Hartford Courant*'s preseason rankings – were back for coach Ed Generali's

Crosby rebounded from its opening loss by defeating Naugatuck, with reserve Greg Hunter scoring 31 points in the 97-82 home win. The Bulldogs then hit 13 three-pointers, including a game-winning buzzer beater from sophomore Jayson Johnson, in a 64-63 triumph at Ansonia. Johnson had 22 points and Tony Ortiz added 13 for Crosby, which trailed by four points in the final minute before rallying for the win.

Ansonia's second loss in three games allowed Holy Cross to claim an early lead in the title race. Ed Generali's Crusaders rolled past Kennedy, 75-48, with big man Edmund Saunders notching a career-high 28 points. Saunders and Harold Miller then combined for 38 points as Holy Cross held off Crosby, 60-48. And Miller netted 24 with Mike Bolton adding 15 in an impressive 90-61 rout of Torrington that enabled Holy Cross to assume top spot in the standings with a 5-0 record.

Ansonia began to turn things around with its own defeat of Torrington, followed by a 60-51 home win over Wilby. Center Len Svelnys registered 24 points, stepped outside the arc to hit three three-pointers and blocked 10 shots as the Chargers held off a late rally to deal Wilby its second league loss of the season.

The result left both Ansonia and Wilby among a quartet of teams with two league losses – along with Kennedy and Torrington – behind undefeated Holy Cross as the midpoint of the regular season approached.

Wilby had the next chance to knock Holy Cross from the unbeaten ranks, and took a four-point lead into the locker room at halftime. But the host Crusaders responded by outscoring the Wildcats 29-13 in the third period, going on to claim a 78-66 victory. Senior guard Harold Miller connected on eight three-pointers and scored a career-high 34 points in the win, while sophomore Ryan Olsen contributed 17 points.

Holy Cross ended the first half of its league campaign with a trip to 7-2 Ansonia, where it had lost the previous two seasons. The Crusaders began the game with a 15-4 spurt before the hosts worked their way back into the game, with 6-7 Phil Mrazik impressing on both ends of the floor to fuel the Chargers' comeback.

With the score tied at 40 in the third quarter, Ansonia scored five straight points to gain control. The lead grew to double digits midway through the final period, but Holy Cross employed a full-court press to storm back late, cutting Ansonia's lead to 61-59 on a Tom Platt layup with 30 seconds left in the game. But that hoop served as the final points

Wilby's DeVonne Parker surpassed the 1,000 point plateau and the 1,000 rebound landmark during his senior season for the Wildcats.

of the contest as Holy Cross couldn't convert on its final possession. Mrazik ended the night with 27 points and Steve Coughlin scored 12 for Ansonia, offsetting 29 points from Harold Miller in pinning a first loss on the Crusaders.

Ansonia's win streak continued with an overtime win over Kennedy in yet another tense NVL battle that went down to the closing seconds. Tight defense, a key feature for both sides on the night, played a role in the closing seconds. A steal by Ansonia's Art Denby led to a pair of free throws by teammate Len Svelnys, giving the host Chargers a 55-52 lead with nine seconds left on the clock.

Hector Maldonado responded for Kennedy by banking in a shot in the lane while getting fouled as the buzzer sounded. The Eagles guard then sank the ensuing foul shot to send the game into overtime tied at 55.

Neither side could pull away in the extra session, with the score knotted again with under a minute remaining. Steve Coughlin, who scored a game-high 23 points, hit one of two free throws with six seconds left to give Ansonia a 62-61 lead, which held as the final scoreline after Armand LeVasseur's last-second attempt didn't fall for Kennedy

Tough-luck Kennedy would find itself on the short end against another front-runner, Holy Cross, the following week. The Eagles employed a deliberate pace to limit Crusader possessions throughout the game, and a game-high 33 points from forward Marlin Parker kept Kennedy within striking distance late in the game.

But Holy Cross' 6-8 sophomore Edmund Saunders – who produced a career-high 29 points and snared ten rebounds – proved to be a major force in the second half. He and guard Harold Miller (20 points) led the way as Holy Cross held

on for a 58-50 road victory and a 12th win of the season.

Ranked fifth in the state after the win, the Crusaders hosted Crosby with UConn coach Jim Calhoun among those in the crowd. Holy Cross started slowly but gained momentum after halftime to cruise past the Bulldogs, who were playing without Jayson Johnson as the sophomore guard was ruled academically ineligible for the rest of the season.

Edmund Saunders (with 28 points) and Harold Miller (with 21) led four Holy Cross players in double figures in the 81-56 win. Chris Latham netted 27 points and Joe Lamonica had 15 for Crosby.

Holy Cross then traveled to Torrington, where it faced a 14-point halftime deficit before turning things around after the intermission. The comeback was led by guard Harold Miller and forward Tom Platt, whose layup tied the game midway through the fourth period.

Torrington regained the lead with under a minute remaining, but an Edmund Saunders' tip-in with two seconds left sent the game to overtime. The Crusaders gained command early in the extra session and held on for a 57-53 win. Miller's 32 points included the 1,000th point of his high school career while Platt finished with 15 points. Rick Koenig paced Torrington with 17 points.

Wilby kept hopes for an NVL title alive by defeating Torrington, Wolcott and Watertown to improve to 11-3 on the season. DeVonne Parker and Terrance Campbell combined for 44 points in the Wildcats' 80-66 comeback victory over Torrington, while Parker grabbed the 1,000th rebound of his high school career in the 70-46 rout of Watertown.

Two more victories brought Wilby's win streak to 8, before Ansonia (at 14-2 in league games) visited the 13-3 Wildcats in a key conference battle. The Chargers claimed control of the contest with a 16-4 run to end the third quarter – capped by Steve Coughlin's three-pointer to beat the period's buzzer – to take a 57-43 advantage into the final quarter.

Coughlin finished with 38 points and helped Len Svelnys and Phil Mrazik control the backboards the rest of the way as Ansonia completed an 81-62 victory – its 14th consecutive win and a fourth straight defeat of Wilby.

The result left just Holy Cross and Ansonia in contention for the league title. With the two teams set to square off in the final week of the regular season, each had a pair of games to maneuver before the expected title clash.

Ansonia stormed past Naugatuck 105-76, with five players hitting double figures, before surviving a late scare against Sacred Heart. Sparked by the shooting of junior guard Mike Sullivan, the Hearts rallied late to cut a double-digit Ansonia lead down to three in the fourth period. But the host Chargers held steady in the closing moments to claim a 63-59 win.

First-place Holy Cross had the tougher of the two remaining schedules. The Crusaders also hit the century mark in defeating Naugatuck, 109-67, with Harold Miller hitting a school-record nine three-pointers, but had to travel to Wilby to maintain its slim lead atop the standings.

After a tight first half, DeVonne Parker and Rodney Cunningham sparked the host Wildcats to a seven-point lead early in the third period. The Crusaders battled back, with Tom Platt and Ryan Olsen contributing while big man Edmund Saunders was on the bench for most of the second half.

The two Crusader forwards scored key hoops in the closing minutes while senior guard Harold Miller – who scored a game-high 31 points – sank eight late free throws as Holy Cross held on for a 71-66 victory.

And so, the Naugatuck Valley League title would once again be decided on the final night of regular season play. Aiming to repeat as conference champion, 18-1 Holy Cross would need to defeat 17-2 Ansonia to avoid a one-game playoff between the two to decide matters.

With Harold Miller hitting from the outside, the host Crusaders built a double-digit lead by the end of the first period. Even with big man Edmund Saunders out of the game with foul trouble against a formidable frontcourt, Holy Cross maintained a 12-point margin at the half, with Miller scoring 24 points before the intermission.

The 5-10 senior guard kept up his torrid shooting after the break as the Crusaders cruised to an 82-65 victory, avenging their only loss of the season to claim a second consecutive NVL crown. Producing a performance for the ages, Miller set school records with ten three-pointers and 51 points.

"It just felt like I was shooting inside of an ocean," Miller told Republican-American reporters after the game. "The more the shots fell, the more I wanted the ball."

Also interviewed after the game, Ansonia's 27-year head coach Tom McQueeney described Miller's performance as "one of the best I've ever seen in a big game. I don't think Anfernee Hardaway could have helped us tonight."

Selected as the fourth seed in the LL division, 19-1 Holy Cross would lead seven NVL schools – four from Waterbury – into the CIAC tournament. At 17-3, Ansonia was seeded second in the Class L bracket, a year after reaching the state semifinals. Wilby and Kennedy were also slotted into the L bracket, as the 6th and 7th seeds.

Wilby's postseason lasted just one game,

Len Svelnys (left) and Phil Mrazik of Ansonia keep Tom Platt of Holy Cross from a rebound during an NVL contest at the Ansonia gym during the 1994-95 season. The two teams would each go on to claim state titles that season.

ousted 72-55 by ninth-seeded Staples of Westport in its opener. Playing a deliberate style, the visitors frustrated the Wildcats and used a third-quarter run to break open a close contest. Peter Van Siclen led Staples' balanced attack with 19 points, while senior DeVonne Parker scored 24 points in his final game for Wilby.

Kennedy impressed in its Class L opener, forcing 36 turnovers and running past Bethel, 92-62. The Eagles' inside-out duo of Armand Levasseur and Marlin Parker combined for 62 points while sophomore Germaine Carr added 17 in the home win – which earned Kennedy a quarterfinal date with league foe Ansonia.

The two teams had split a pair of one-point victories regular-season contests. Yet the tournament matchup played on a neutral court at Naugatuck High looked to be a blowout early, as the formidable Chargers scored 15 of the game's first 17 points.

But Kennedy fought back throughout the middle periods, tightening its defense and closing to within four points of Ansonia in the third quarter. The Eagles' Marlin Parker notched his 1,000th career point during the second-half comeback that ultimately fell short, as Ansonia held on for a 65-58 victory. Steve Coughlin, Phil Mrazik and Len Svelnys all hit double figures for 19-3 Ansonia, while Armand Levasseur's 24 points paced Kennedy.

Ansonia's three big men led the way again in the next round, a 62-53 triumph over Bassick of Bridgeport after trailing by five at halftime. The Chargers scored 16 of the game's final 18 points in the semifinal win to claim a place in the Class L championship game against top seed St. Joseph of Trumbull – 20 years after the school's only other appearance in a CIAC title game.

St. Joseph, playing in its eight state final in 11 years, had the advantage of experience on the big stage. But Ansonia had the size advantage, which proved to be the difference in a game where neither team had more than a five-point lead at any point.

Six-foot-eight center Len Svelnys, who notched 31 points and 19 rebounds for the game, hit a jumper to break a tie in the final minute and later sank two free throws to seal a 56-54 Ansonia victory. Svelnys was named the game's most valuable player for the 21-3 Chargers, who claimed a first-ever state title in basketball, three months after its football team won a CIAC Class SS championship.

Two of the three teams that handed Ansonia defeats during the season met in the first round of the LL tournament. Holy Cross hosted city rival Crosby, who had lost guard Jayson Johnson midway through the campaign yet still qualified for the postseason with a 9-11 record.

Chris Latham – who had shouldered the scoring load for coach Nick Augelli's troops in Johnson's absence – started the CIAC tourney game well, connecting on a number of jumpers as the underdog Bulldogs opened a 22-15 lead in the second period.

Harold Miller

But Holy Cross recovered from its slow start and grabbed the lead by halftime, with 6-8 sophomore Edmund Saunders beginning to impose himself on both ends of the court. Crusader senior Harold Miller then sparked a third-quarter spurt by hitting four three-pointers, and Holy Cross pulled away for an 84-54 home win. Miller and Saunders accounted for 51 Crusader points, while Latham led Crosby with 24 points.

Holy Cross's second-round game against Southington was a physical affair. Saunders netted a game-high 25 points and the Crusaders received solid contributions from substitutes Bill Horrigan and Wes Pilon in securing a 70-59 victory.

Saunders elevated his game even further against Fitch High of Groton in the quarterfinals, scoring 16 of a career-high 40 points in the first period as Holy Cross cruised past the fifth seed. Forced away from the basket, the 6-8 sophomore hit a number of midrange jumpers to open up the game for the versatile Crusaders, who were able to outrace the speedy Fitch side as the game progressed into a fast-paced affair. Miller netted 15 of his 28 points in the second half of the 98-71 win – sending Holy Cross to the state semifinals for the third time in coach Ed Generali's first seven seasons at the helm.

And with six minutes left in the semi against Westhill of Stamford, it seemed that the Crusaders' season would again end one game short of the CIAC final. Featuring its own stellar inside-outside combination in Stephen Armstead and Jamar Dunmore, Westhill built up a ten-point lead a couple of minutes into the final period.

Displaying the type of grit and determination worthy of championship sides, Holy Cross staged a dramatic comeback to send the game into overtime. Tom Platt scored 10 of his 15 points in the fourth quarter to key the late surge, which was capped by a buzzer-beating layup by Edmund Saunders following a Harold Miller miss after a court-length drive.

Having gained a new life, Holy Cross took command in the extra session. Saunders scored seven of his 30 points, the defense made early stops, and the Crusaders held on for an 82-81 win. Miller added 26 for the 23-1 Crusaders – helping to offset the combined 56 points from the Westhill duo of Armstead and Dunmore – while contributions from complementary players such as Platt and Lucas Markelon proved crucial to victory.

Standing in the way of a second state title for the Waterbury school was second-ranked Windsor, which had knocked Holy Cross out of the previous year's tournament via a 77-75 second-round decision.

The first half of the LL final at Central Connecticut's Detrick gymnasium was a tight affair, with Windsor's Keyon Smith and Russell Scott leading a second-quarter run that gave the second-seeded Warriors a 32-27 halftime lead.

Windsor's advantage reached 10 points early in the third quarter, before Holy Cross began to cut away at the lead. Defense and the rise of a complementary player proved key to the Crusaders late rally in the semifinals, and the theme applied yet again in the championship game.

This time, it was forward Mike Bolton who stepped up, netting 14 points – twice his average – to complement the scoring of Miller and Saunders. The deficit was down to two points early in the fourth period, before Scott hit two free throws to give Windsor a 49-45 lead with just over six minutes remaining.

Amazingly, that would be Windsor's only points of the final period as the Holy Cross defense clamped down in the closing minutes. A Harold Miller three-pointer from the top of the key gave the Crusaders their first lead of the second half at the 4:19 mark, turning the tide for good.

Miller would score eight of the last 12 points for Holy Cross and finish with 21 points and five assists in the 57-49 victory. The senior guard was named the game's

most valuable player for his efforts in guiding the Crusaders to the school's second CIAC state title.

"Great players, when the game's on the line, they find a way to win and that's what Harold did for us," said coach Ed Generali to *Hartford Courant* writer Kevin Hayes after the game.

"I told the kids after the third quarter that they could either dig in and come back or start looking forward to next year," he continued. "They sucked it up and that's a tribute to the determination that these kids had."

Generali's squad finished the season with the number-one ranking in Connecticut in both the *New Haven Register*'s and *Hartford Courant*'s Top Ten polls (with Manchester and St. Joseph of Trumbull ousted from tourney play). The NVL's Ansonia was ranked second in the Courant poll.

'It's great to know we've gotten the respect of the coaches (*Courant* poll) and the writers (*Register* poll)," said Generali, who became the first person to coach two different Waterbury schools to CIAC state basketball titles. "It is a fitting end to a dream season."

Harold Miller – who had signed to play college basketball at Northeastern University – was named to the New Haven Register's All-State team. The senior guard was one of three players named to both the All-City and All-NVL teams, along with DeVonne Parker of Wilby and Kennedy's Marlin Parker.

Crosby's Chris Latham and Kennedy's Armand LeVasseur rounded out the All-City first team, while Ansonia's Steve Coughlin and Joe Carrafiello of Seymour joined Miller and the two Parkers on the All-NVL first team.

Looking Back: Saunders, Miller and Generali reflect on Holy Cross' 1994-95 Class LL title

The stars of Holy Cross High's run to the 1994-95 Class LL state title each consider a couple of previous losses as the impetus for the team ultimately cutting down the nets after a successful championship journey.

For guard Harold Miller, it was an early-season loss at Ansonia that sparked an incredible personal run to end the season.

Big man Edmund Saunders' memory goes back to the prior season and a season-ending loss to Windsor in the state tourney.

"The championship run in 1995 was great, especially after I messed it up for the senior class the year before when I missed two late free throws in our tourney loss," recalls Saunders, who to-gether with his teammates gained some revenge on Windsor, winning 57-49 in the 1995 title game.

"I had a chip on my shoulder from the way the previous season ended, and I was ready to play," adds Saunders. "Having played the summer with coach Jim Salmon and Paterson Catholic in a number of competitions really helped me."

The Crusaders had won the Nau-gatuck Valley League the previous season but had lost All-City performer Paul Nardozzi and Derek Gray to graduation. Despite the losses in per-sonnel, Generali had molded another solid team "where everyone knew their roles," according to Saunders.

"We had a great coach in Mr. Gen-erali, a great point guard in Harold Miller, and Tom Platt and Mike Bolton provided the toughness for the team,"

says Saunders. "As long as Mike and Tom showed up, we were going to win. They did things that didn't show in the stat sheet."

Miller, the team's senior lead guard, says "the whole team bought into Coach G's philosophy. I truly feel we needed every single member of the team to win it that year. Our role play-ers were huge all the way down to the championship game."

Defense was a focus for the 1994-95 team, according to Miller. "Some games were pretty ugly but we were relentless on defense.... we were always ready to dig in on defense. And Ed (Saunders) was arguably the best defender I have seen since Marcus Camby!"

Holy Cross cruised through the first half of the 1994-95 regular season, which included some impressive wins over city rivals. "Considering the way we handled some teams, we knew we had what it takes to make a run for the state title," recalls Saunders, who sur-passed his career high for points three times in the Crusaders' first 12 games of his sophomore season.

The Crusaders regrouped after a mid-season loss at Ansonia, with the return matchup between the two at Holy Cross serving as the NVL title decider. Miller produced a performance for the ages in that contest, setting school re-cord for three-pointers (10) and points (51) as the host Crusaders claimed an 82-65 victory and a second consecutive league crown.

"The loss to Ansonia earlier in the season was the turning point for me," recalls Miller. "It was a tough loss, but credit to them for making us play terrible...they were as good as us on defense and could get it going on offense. (Shout out to Lenny Svelnys and Steve Coughlin aka 'Stanford Steve'!)"

Ansonia ended up being ranked among the top teams in the state and eventually won the Class L state championship, indicative of their talent and ability, notes Miller. "But that loss gave me major confidence that we could beat them next time and we could win the state if we played a little bit better.

"I went on this run where I had 8 three-pointers and 34 points versus Wilby, 9 threes and 39 points versus Naugatuck, and then 10 threes and 51 points versus Ansonia for the NVL championship," he adds. "I was in a groove and was determined to win the states that year."

The postseason began with an opening-round defeat of city foe Crosby, with Miller and Saunders combining for 51 points. Two rounds later, the 6-8 sophomore center notched a career-high 40 points as Holy Cross ousted Fitch of Groton in the quarterfinals.

"The toughest game in the tournament was against Westhill (of Stamford) in the semifinals," says Saunders. "Windsor was tough in the final, but I believed that whoever won our semifinal would go on to win the championship."

Holy Cross was down by ten points in the fourth period, but staged a dramatic comeback to send the game to overtime. Platt scored 10 points in that rally, capped by Saunders' follow of a Miller miss that beat the buzzer to tie the game and force the extra session.

Generali's Crusaders gained control in

overtime and held on to outlast Westhill, 82-81, and earn a place in the LL title game against Windsor.

"Ed's tip-in versus Westhill saved our season," believes Miller. "His offense just continued to flourish each game; he had some of his best offensive games the deeper we went into the season."

In the final, "Harold really carried us as I didn't play for most the whole first half," remembers Saunders, who picked up some early fouls. "Thank God everyone stepped up that game and did more."

Harold Miller

Bolton proved his worth by contributing 14 points, while the Crusader defense held Windsor to two points in the fourth quarter to rally for the 57-49 victory. Miller scored 8 of his team's final 12 points to finish with 21 on the night and earn most valuable player honors.

"The 1995 team was really special. We had this mantra of "Refuse to Lose" and we stuck to it the entire season," remembers Miller, who acknowledges his coaches at Holy Cross. "From Coach Generali, and the entire coaching staff – Coach Frank Steponaitis, Coach Ken 'Smooth' Sinclair, and Coach Mike Phelan – they were an amazing staff!"

Miller enjoyed a fine college career at Northeastern University, captaining the team his senior season. "We did not win as many games as I would have liked but I ended up scoring over 1000 points, and won the Reggie Lewis Award as a senior."

Invited to pro/combine camps, Miller had a couple of surgeries on his plantar fascia and also ended up slipping a disc in his back, so he did not play pro ball.

"In a weird way, the injuries kind of saved my life because I was forced to buckle down with school and a career. I earned a Bachelor's Degree in Sociology, Master's Degree in Education and am currently working on a Doctorate Degree in Law & Policy - all from Northeastern University!"

He has since served in Boston's public school system, and became a teacher, coach, assistant principal, principal and interim assistant superintendent. "I am now back in school full-time working on my doctorate, consulting, coaching girls' soccer and working on a few other projects."

While he has many family members still in Waterbury, Miller lives with his wife and daughter in Boston.

"I believe health and education are the key to life," says Miller. "It is not as much about degrees but more so following your passion, always doing your homework and research and being the best person you can be each day!"

While falling short of another state title in his final two years at Holy Cross, Saunders would go on to lead the Crusaders to two more NVL titles with the Crusaders. He went on to play at UConn, winning a national championship when the Huskies defeated Duke, 77-74, for the 1999 NCAA title.

After college, Saunders went on to play professionally in South America

Edmund Saunders and UConn teammates Kevin Freeman and Richard Hamilton with the 1999 NCAA trophy, on the 20th anniversary of the school's first national championship.

and Europe for eight years. "I now work for the State of Connecticut," adds Saunders. "My wife and I have a foundation called Brass City Cares. We do events for the community throughout the year, just trying to give back and help those in need."

Looking back to his high school days, Saunders' fondest memories include the city rivalries, building bonds with teammates, and the run to the 1994-95 CIAC championship. "That 1995 team was special," he says. "We just had a great team and everyone got along."

One "special" note about that 1995 title is that is marked the first (and thus far only) time someone had coached two different Waterbury schools to CIAC state basketball championships.

Ed Generali, who guided Sacred Heart to the 1984 Class M title, thus made history with the 1995 championship for Holy Cross, which earned the Crusaders the number-one ranking among state teams after the victory.

"It is a fitting end to a dream season," noted Generali in his post game comments to the *Hartford Courant*. In praising Miller's MVP performance, Generali added: "Great players, when the game's on the line, they find a way to win and that's what Harold did for us."

Generali would lead the Crusaders to one more state title, in 2000, when Holy Cross topped Bassick of Bridgeport, 74-50, for the Class L championship.

In addition to the state crowns, Generali's most memorable moments and games at the Holy Cross gym during his coaching career include "the 1995 NVL title decider against Ansonia in front of a raucous crowd at The Pit," when Miller scored 51 points, including 10 three-pointers, as the host Crusaders pulled away for an 82-65 win.

Others include:

■ a CIAC Class LL encounter with Wilbur Cross of New Haven in 1991, "when Rob Paternostro hit a driving layup before the final buzzer for a 63-61 win that avenged a loss the season before and gave him 1,000 points for his career."

■ "The come-from-behind, overtime win over Sacred Heart in 1997, after being down 6 points with 40 seconds left in regulation," says Generali. "The two teams were undefeated and ranked numbers 1 and 2 in New England (according to a NESN poll). It was just an incredible game, and the player who hit a huge three-pointer in the comeback is now Holy Cross coach, Ryan Olsen."

Ironically, Generali admits he "hated going to 'The Pit' as a visiting coach, but so loved being there as the home school coach. The dim lighting there really added to its aura, and I was actually disappointed when new efficient lighting was installed!" he says.

Holy Cross fans wouldn't be disappointed much during Generali's tenure, which lasted through the 2015-16 season. Building on the foundation begun by Tim McDonald, Generali's Crusader teams won 493 games over 27 seasons, and captured eight NVL titles in addition to the two state championships.

Four years after the Holy Cross gymnasium was named in McDonald's honor, the school officially dedicated the playing floor as "Coach Ed Generali Court" in 2017.

"I am honestly so blessed to have coached at two great institutions and have the players that I had play for me," says Generali. "Then to actually have the court named after me was surreal. And it happened the year after the Boys' and Girls' Club of Greater Waterbury named their court after my father, Mario, the longtime director there How many people can say that?"

The best part of the ceremony, adds Generali, "was that it came on a Friday night, before a game against a city opponent. When coaching, I said for years to my players that there is no better place to be than in the Tim McDonald gym on a Friday night for a game against a city opponent – and that held true that night."

161

NVL Boys Basketball Champions

2021	Sacred Heart		1996	Holy Cross
2020	Naugatuck		1995	Holy Cross
2019	Sacred Heart		1994	Holy Cross
2018	Sacred Heart		1993	Wilby
2017	Sacred Heart		1992	Wilby
2016	Sacred Heart		1991	Kennedy
2015	Sacred Heart		1990	Kennedy
2014	Crosby		1989	Kennedy
2013	Crosby		1988	Holy Cross
2012	Watertown		1987	Crosby
2011	Crosby		1986	Wilby
2010	Crosby		1985	Crosby
2009	Crosby		1984	Sacred Heart
2008	Crosby		1983	Ansonia
2007	Crosby, Holy Cross, Torrington		1982	Crosby
2006	Crosby		1981	Holy Cross
2005	Crosby		1980	Sacred Heart
2004	Crosby		1979	Holy Cross
2003	Sacred Heart		1978	Crosby
2002	Sacred Heart		1977	Holy Cross
2001	Holy Cross		1976	Holy Cross
2000	Holy Cross		1975	Crosby
1999	Holy Cross		1974	Wilby
1998	Crosby		1973	Holy Cross
1997	Holy Cross		1972	Kennedy

Contributed / Sacred Heart High School

The 1983-84 Naugatuck Vallley League champion Sacred Heart team.

1972-73 NVL champion Holy Cross Crusaders

1971	Sacred Heart		1951	Ansonia, Crosby
1970	Sacred Heart		1950	Ansonia
1969	Naugatuck		1949	Torrington
1968	Wilby		1948	Torrington
1967	Sacred Heart		1947	Leavenworth
1966	Crosby		1946	Naugatuck
1965	Sacred Heart		1945	Naugatuck
1964	Croft, Sacred Heart		1944	Torrington
1963	Croft, Sacred Heart		1943	Warren Harding
1962	Ansonia		1942	Torrington, Warren Harding
1961	Croft, Crosby		1941	Torrington
1960	Naugatuck		1940	Naugatuck
1959	Naugatuck		1939	Naugatuck, Torrington
1958	Crosby, Torrington		1938	Naugatuck
1957	Naugatuck		1937	Warren Harding
1956	Naugatuck, Sacred Heart		1936	Bridgeport Central, Torrington
1955	Naugatuck		1935	Bridgeport Central
1954	Crosby, Torrington		1934	Bridgeport Central
1953	Torrington		1933	Bridgeport Central
1952	Ansonia, Torrington, Wilby		1932	Naugatuck

Billy Finn Award Winners

2021	Zion Lott, WCA	1991	Jerome Malloy, Kennedy
2020	Justin Davis, Crosby	1990	Anthony Banks, Wilby
2019	Marquan Watson, WCA	1989	Wayne Boyette, Crosby
2018	Isiah Gaiter, Sacred Heart	1988	Phil Lott, Wilby
2017	Jeremiah Kendall, Crosby	1987	Kevin Eason, Wilby
2016	Mustapha Heron, Sacred Heart	1986	Willie Davis, Crosby
2015	Don Jarrett, Kennedy	1985	Kelly Monroe, Holy Cross
2014	Tyshon Rogers, Crosby	1984	Anthony Perry, Sacred Heart
2013	Walter Wright, Wilby	1983	Marty Hayre, Wilby
2012	Michael Mallory, Holy Cross	1982	Carmen Giampetruzzi, Holy Cross
2011	Marvin Hampton, Crosby	1981	Bernie Ireland, Crosby
2010	Ryan Kolb, Holy Cross	1980	Ken Sinclair, Sacred Heart
2009	Anthony Ireland, Crosby	1979	Spencer Harrison, Holy Cross
2008	B.J. Monteiro, Crosby	1978	Mark White, Crosby
2007	Lee Brockett, Kennedy	1977	Clay Johnson, Holy Cross
2006	Damian Saunders, Crosby	1976	Steve Johnson, Crosby
2005	James Moore, Crosby	1975	Jim Abromaitis, Holy Cross
2004	Jon Lucky, Sacred Heart	1974	Lou Canady, Wilby
2003	Moe Chisholm, Wilby	1973	Tony Hanson, Holy Cross
2002	Rob Lucky, Sacred Heart	1972	Tom Dupont, Wilby
2001	Mark Konecny, Holy Cross	1971	Gary Franks, Sacred Heart
2000	Ryan Gomes, Wilby	1970	Glenn Cantin, Crosby
1999	Marvin Rountree, Crosby	1969	Joel Goldson, Sacred Heart
1998	Will Stenson, Wilby	1968	Art Williams, Wilby
1997	Edmund Saunders, Holy Cross	1967	Don Sasso, Sacred Heart
1996	Marlin Parker, Kennedy	1966	John Sinclair, Crosby
1995	Harold Miller, Holy Cross	1965	E.J. Harty, Sacred Heart
1994	Mike Sanders, Sacred Heart	1964	Joe Gillis, Sacred Heart
1993	Marcus Robinson, Wilby	1963	Art Moore, Wilby
1992	Garnett Petteway, Kennedy		

Contributed / Crosby High School

Justin Davis, 2020 winner of the Billy Finn Award, brings the ball upcourt against John Greene in a Holy Cross- Crosby game in 2019-2020.

Waterbury's 2,000-Point Club

The top five scorers in Waterbury high school history have all eclipsed 2,000 points in their scholastic careers:

1) Tyshon Rogers, Crosby ....2,292 points
2) Phil Lott, Wilby .... 2,230 points
3) Jerome Malloy, Kennedy .... 2,124 points
4) Edmund Saunders, Holy Cross .... 2,087 points
5) Mustapha Heron, Sacred Heart .... 2,056 points

1,000-Point Scorers for NVL-Member City Schools (who graduated between 1971 and 1995)

(the time period covered in this book)

Crosby:
Steve Johnson 1,494
Harun Ramey 1,448
Wayne Boyette 1,401
Willie Davis 1,045

Holy Cross:
Kelly Monroe 1,447
Spencer Harrison 1,290
Harold Miller 1,286
Brian Davis 1,243
Tony Hanson 1,222
Mike Robinson 1,205
Carmen Giampetruzzi 1,193
Clay Johnson 1,183
Rob Paternostro 1,028

Kennedy:
Jerome Malloy 2,123
Marlin Parker 1,557
Lamar Powell 1,245
Garnett Petteway 1,171
Malik Williams 1,069
Waddel Walton 1,013

Sacred Heart:
Mike Sanders 1,635
Gary Franks 1,110
Pete Eason 1,068
Bob Moffo 1,014
Anthony Perry 1,007

Wilby:
Phil Lott 2,230
Marcus Robinson 1,561
DeVonne Parker 1,550
Terrence Lott 1,122
Manny Wright 1,114
Kevin Eason 1,035
Keith Lott 1,024

All-State Performers for City Schools
(selected by the New Haven Register)
(for the time period covered in this book)

Crosby:
Steve Johnson (Class L, 1976)
Bernie Ireland (Class L, 1981)
Brian Jones (Class L, 1982)
Willie Davis (Class L, 1986)
Wayne Boyette (1989)
Harun Ramey (1990)
　　　　　(1991)

Holy Cross:
Tony Hanson (Class L, 1972)
　　　　　(Class LL, 1973)
Jim Abromaitis (Class LL, 1975)
Clay Johnson (Class LL, 1977)
Spencer Harrison (Class LL, 1979)
Bruce Johnson (Class LL, 1981)
Carmen Giampetruzzi (Class LL, 1982)
Kelly Monroe (Class LL, 1984)
　　　　　(Class LL, 1985)
Lamarr Stinson (Class LL, 1988)
Brian Davis (1993)
Harold Miller (1995)

Kennedy:
Jerome Malloy (1990)
　　　　　(1991)
Garnett Petteway (1992)

Kaynor Tech:
Larry Dawson (Class M, 1971)
Chris White (Class L, 1977)
Rufus Freeman (Class L, 1985)
　　　　　(Class L, 1986)

Sacred Heart:
Gary Franks (Class L, 1971)
Anthony Perry (Class M, 1984)

Wilby:
Marty Hayre (Class L, 1983)
Phil Lott (Class M, 1987)
　　　　　(Class L, 1988)
Manny Wright (1992)
Marcus Robinson (1993)